Presented To:

_____

Presented By:

_____

Date:

_____

God's
Devotional
Book

FOR TEENS

HONOR HB BOOKS

Inspiration and Motivation for the Seasons of Life

An Imprint of Cook Communications Ministries • Colorado Springs, CO

10 9 8 7 6 5   1 2 3 4 5

God's Devotional Book for Teens
ISBN 1-56292-516-4

Copyright © 2005 by Honor Books,
An Imprint of Cook Communications Ministries
4050 Lee Vance View
Colorado Springs, CO

Developed by Bordon Books
6532 E. 71st Street, Ste. 105
Tulsa, OK 74133

Original Manuscript prepared by W.B. Freeman Concepts
Compilation and Composition of new elements by Linda Holland in association
with Snapdragon Editorial Group, Inc.
Interior designed by Jackson Design Co.

Introduction

You're not yet an adult, but you're not really a kid anymore, either. You may be twelve or thirteen and just beginning the teen years—fifteen or sixteen and about to get your driver's license; or seventeen or eighteen and about to graduate from high school. These are the years someone once called the "tween" years.

In today's high-pressure, fast-paced world, it's not easy being a teenager. You're faced with difficult situations every day. Friends and peers may pressure you to do things you don't want to do. They may pressure you to do things you think you might want to do but know you shouldn't. What you need is the strength, resolve, and encouragement to pass up those temporarily enticing and exciting things in order to work toward God's destiny for your life.

God does have a plan for your life. His plan is a good one. He has a plan for you to prosper. His plan will give you hope and a bright future. (See Jeremiah 29:11.) *God's Devotional Book for Teens* was designed to encourage and inspire you to discover, desire, and implement God's divine plan for your life. The powerful quotes and Scriptures will give you something on which to meditate, and the devotional stories will help you to apply their principles. Is life challenging? Sure . . . but with God's help and guidance, your future is great!

STICK TO IT

In March of 1987, Eamon Coughlan was running in a qualifying heat at the World Indoor Track Championships in Indianapolis. The Irishman was the reigning world record-holder at fifteen hundred meters, and he was favored to win the race handily. Unfortunately, with two-and-a-half laps left to run, he was tripped and fell hard. Even so, he got up and with great effort, he managed to catch the race leaders. With only twenty yards to go, he was in third place, which would have been good enough to qualify for the final race.

Then Couglan looked over his shoulder to the inside. Seeing no one there, he relaxed his effort slightly. What he hadn't noticed, however, was that a runner was charging hard on the outside. This runner passed Couglan just a yard before the finish line, thus eliminating him from the finals.

Coughlan's great comeback effort ended up being worthless for one and only one reason: he momentarily took his eyes off the finish line and focused on the would-be competitors instead.

One of the most important factors in reaching your goals in life is to have single-minded focus. Don't let yourself become distracted by what others do or say. Run your race to win!

> CONSIDER THE POSTAGE STAMP:
> ITS USEFULNESS CONSISTS IN THE ABILITY TO STICK TO ONE THING TILL IT GETS THERE.
>
> JOSH BILLINGS

I HAVE FOUGHT THE GOOD FIGHT, I HAVE FINISHED THE RACE, I HAVE KEPT THE FAITH.
2 TIMOTHY 4:7 NIV

WISE WORDS

Do you not know that in a race the
runners all compete, but only one receives the prize? Run in such a
way that you may win it. Athletes
exercise self-control in all things;
they do it to receive a perishable
wreath, but we an imperishable
one. So I do not run aimlessly, nor
do I box as though beating the air;
but I punish my body and enslave it,
so that after proclaiming to others I
myself should not be disqualified.

1 CORINTHIANS 9:24-27 NRSV

When a man is gloomy,
EVERYTHING
seems to go wrong;
when he is cheerful,
everything seems right!

PROVERBS 15:15 TLB

A CHEERFUL ATTITUDE MAKES EVERYTHING BETTER

A LITTLE BOY WAS ONCE overheard talking to himself as he strutted out of his house into the backyard, carrying a baseball and bat. Once in the yard, he tipped his baseball cap to his eager puppy; and picking up the bat and ball, he announced with a loud voice, "I'm the greatest hitter in the world!"

He then proceeded to toss the ball into the air, swing at it, and miss. "Strike one!" he cried, as if playing the role of umpire.

He picked up the ball, threw it into the air, and said again, "I'm the greatest baseball hitter ever!" Again he swung at the ball and missed. "Strike two!" he announced to his dog and the yard.

Undaunted, he picked up the ball, examined his bat, and then just before tossing the ball into the air, announced once again, "I'm the greatest hitter who ever lived!" He swung the bat hard but missed the ball for the third time. "Strike three!" he cried. Then he added, "Wow! What a pitcher! I'm the greatest pitcher in all the world!"

A positive mental attitude goes a long way toward making a difficult job seem small.

Who's Who:

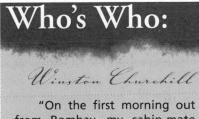

Winston Churchill

"On the first morning out from Bombay, my cabin-mate and I woke up early and began to chat cheerfully to each other," Colonel H.A. Irvine recalled years later. "From the opposite cabin came a peevish cry of 'Stop that noise!' We naturally decided to investigate.

"Scowling at us from a lower bunk was a very youthful person clad in a beautiful pair of pink pajamas. Smart and I said nothing; but we each took hold of a foot. Whilst he voyaged up and down the cook's galley on his back, we realized that our victim, though his language would have done no credit to a present-day BBC announcer, was a born orator.

"And he was; for his name was Winston Churchill."

WALK JUSTLY
AND LOVE MERCY

> ## ALL VIRTUE IS SUMMED UP IN DEALING JUSTLY.
> ARISTOTLE

TO CRACK THE lily-white system of higher education in Georgia in the 1960s, black leaders decided they needed to find only two squeaky-clean students who couldn't be challenged on moral, intellectual, or educational grounds. In a discussion about who might be chosen, Alfred Holmes immediately volunteered his son, Hamilton, the top black male senior in the city. Charlayne Hunter-Gault also stepped forward and expressed an interest in applying to the university. Georgia delayed admitting both boys on grounds it had no room in its dormitories, and the matter eventually ended up in federal court. Judge Bootle ordered the university to admit the two, who were qualified in every respect; and thus, segregation ended at the university level in that state and soon the nation.

Attorney General Robert Kennedy declared in a speech not long after: "We know that it is the law which enables men to live together, that creates order out of chaos. . . . And we know that if one man's rights are denied, the rights of all are endangered."

Justice may be universal, but it always begins at the individual level. Is there someone that you might treat more justly today?

What does the LORD require of you
but to do justly, to love mercy,
and to walk humbly with your God?

MICAH 6:8 NKJV

TOP **10** TIPS for Living Justly

1. SHOW MERCY TO ALL.

2. DEMONSTRATE FAIRNESS IN YOUR ACTIONS.

3. TREAT EVERYONE THE SAME.

4. ASSUME A HUMBLE SPIRIT.

5. CHECK PREJUDICES AT THE DOOR.

6. DON'T BE RUDE.

7. DO YOUR BEST TO GET ALONG WITH OTHERS.

8. DON'T HOLD A GRUDGE.

9. DEFEND THOSE WHO CAN'T DEFEND THEMSELVES.

10. EXHIBIT GOD'S LOVE.

CONSIDER
THIS!

How Do You Spell Servant?

Submit yourself to God and to others.

Elevate the importance of others.

Remember to maintain the heart of a servant.

Value all people equally.

Assume a humble position.

Never forget that Christ came to serve.

Treat others as you would want to be treated.

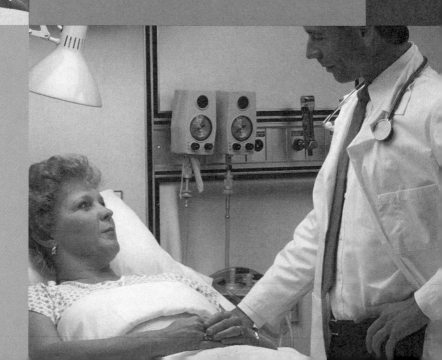

DOWN TO EARTH

People often think of heart surgeons as being the arrogant prima donnas of the medical world. Those who know Dr. William DeVries, the surgeon who pioneered the artificial heart, couldn't disagree more. Co-workers at Humana Hospital Audubon in Louisville, Kentucky, describe DeVries as the kind of doctor who shows up on Sundays just to cheer up discouraged patients. He occasionally changes dressings, traditionally considered a nurse's job; and if a patient wants him to stick around and talk, he always does.

Friends say DeVries is an old shoe who fits in wherever he goes. He likes to wear cowboy boots

> **IT NEEDS MORE SKILL THAN I CAN TELL TO PLAY THE SECOND FIDDLE WELL.**

with his surgical scrubs, and he often repairs hearts to the beat of Vivaldi or jazz. "He has always got a smile lurking," says Louisville cardiologist Dr. Robert Goodin, "and he's always looking for a way to let it out."

No matter how high you rise, never forget that you started out at ground zero. Even if you were born to great wealth and privilege, you still were born as a helpless babe. Real success comes not in thinking you have arrived at a place where others should serve you, but in recognizing that in whatever place you are, you have arrived at a position where you can serve others.

Do you want to stand out? Then step down. Be a servant.

MATTHEW 23:11 MSG

USE YOUR TALENTS TO GLORIFY GOD

The German sculptor, Dannaker, worked for two years on a statue of Christ until it looked perfect to him. He called a little girl into his studio, and pointing to the statue, he asked her, "Who is that?" The little girl promptly replied, "A great man."

Dannaker was disheartened. He took his chisel and began anew. For six long years, he toiled. Again, he invited a little girl into his workshop, stood her before the figure, and said, "Who is that?" She looked up at it for a moment, and then tears welled up in her eyes as she folded her hands across her chest and said, "Suffer the little children to come unto me" (Mark 10:14). This time Dannaker knew he had succeeded.

> **Only passions,** great passions, can elevate the soul to great things.
> DENIS DIDEROT

The sculptor later confessed that during those six years, Christ had revealed himself to him in a vision, and he had only transferred to the marble what he had seen with his inner eyes.

Later, when Napoleon Bonaparte asked him to make a statue of Venus for the Louvre, Dannaker refused. "A man," he said, "who has seen Christ can never employ his gifts in carving a pagan goddess. My art is henceforth a consecrated thing."

The true value of a work comes not from effort, nor its completion, but from Christ who inspires it.

[Be] fervent in spirit, serving the Lord.

ROMANS 12:11 NKJV

☑ JUST DO IT

#1 **Wisdom tells us that God plants a seed of passion inside each of us in order to fulfill our destiny on Earth. To discover your passion, answer the following questions:**

#2
- What is your yearning? It's a feeling that pulls and attracts you like a magnet toward a preferred activity.
- What deeply satisfies you? This will be something you get a kick out of doing.

#3
- What is easy for you to learn? You get it. It makes sense to you. You learn it eagerly and easily.

#4
- You feel moments when you are in the "zone." At times it feels natural to you. You can imagine yourself doing this activity and doing it well. You sense a flow.

#5

#6

#7

#8

#9

Fun Facts

The scribes who copied the Old Testament Scriptures had their work cut out for them! Consider this:

The Old Testament contains:

- 39 books
- 929 chapters
- 23,214 verses
- 593,493 words

Imagine what dedication it took to make even one full copy?

LEAVE A LASTING MARK

The **greatest** use of life is to **spend** it for
something that will **outlast** it.
William James

Although we do not have the original manuscripts of the New Testament, we do have more than 99.9 percent of the original text because of the faithful work of manuscript copyists over the centuries.

Copying was a long, arduous process. In ancient days, copyists did not sit at desks while writing, but rather stood or made copies while sitting on benches or stools, holding a scroll on their knees. Notes at the end of some scrolls tell of the drudgery of the work:

"He who does not know how to write supposes it to be no labor; but though only three fingers write, the whole body labors."

"Writing bows one's back, thrusts the ribs into one's stomach, and fosters a general debility."

"As travelers rejoice to see their home country, so also is the end of a book to those who toil."

Even so, without the work of faithful copyists, we would not have the Christian Scriptures today. As one scribe aptly noted: "There is no scribe who will not pass away, but what his hands have written will remain forever."

If you truly want your work to last, do work that touches the eternal truth and nature of God.

Jesus said, "Store up for yourselves treasures in heaven, where moth and rust do not destroy, and where thieves do not break in and steal."

MATTHEW 6:20 NIV

ONLY SPEAK WELL OF OTHERS

After several months of romance, Napoleon and Josephine decided to marry. The notary who made out the marriage contract was one of Josephine's friends. He secretly advised her against marrying "an obscure little officer who has nothing besides his uniform and sword and has no future." He thought she should find someone of greater worth. With her charms, he advised, she might attract a wealthy man, perhaps an army contractor or a business investor.

Napoleon was in the next room while the notary was giving this advice to his beloved. He could hear every word that was said. Still, he did not disclose he had overheard. Years later, however, he had his revenge.

After his coronation as Emperor, this same notary appeared before him on a matter of business. At the conclusion of their appointment, Napoleon smiled and observed that Madame de Beauharnais—now that she was queen of France—had done very well, after all, to have married that "obscure little officer who possessed nothing besides his uniform and sword and had no future."

The notary was forced to agree that Madame, indeed, had done well. As for himself, he was still a notary!

Be careful before you pass judgment on another. You're revealing something about yourself, and your words may come back to bite you.

> A MAN NEVER DISCLOSES HIS OWN CHARACTER SO CLEARLY AS WHEN HE DESCRIBES ANOTHER'S.
>
> JEAN PAUL RICHTER

THE GOOD MAN BRINGS GOOD THINGS OUT OF THE GOOD STORED UP IN HIM, AND THE EVIL MAN BRINGS EVIL THINGS OUT OF THE EVIL STORED UP IN HIM.

MATTHEW 12:35 NIV

WISE WORDS

Why is it that the good things people say about us never give as much permanent pleasure as the bad things they say about us give us enduring pain; and that the glow of praise quickly dims and must be continually replenished, while the barbs of dispraise rankle for an unconscionably long time?

SYDNEY HARRIS

HOW Do YOU MEASURE Up?

How self-disciplined are you?

A. I play sports on a regular basis.

B. I exercise at least three times a week.

C. I limit my intake of junk food.

D. I push myself to excel beyond my previous successes.

E. I challenge myself to attempt activities I've never tried before.

F. I attempt tasks that seem too difficult.

G. I believe I can do all things through Christ who strengthens me.

H. I force myself to go to bed at a reasonable hour.

I. I keep my commitments.

J. I get to school on time.

K. I obey my parents, even when I don't agree with them.

SELF-DISCIPLINE
CAN HELP YOU OVERCOME

WHAT WE DO ON SOME GREAT OCCASION WILL PROBABLY DEPEND ON WHAT WE ALREADY ARE; AND WHAT WE ARE WILL BE THE RESULT OF PRECIOUS YEARS OF SELF-DISCIPLINE.

H. P. LIDDON

During a homecoming football game against rival Concordia, Augsburg College found itself losing miserably. Late in the fourth quarter, however, noseguard David Stevens came off the bench and sparked a fire. He initiated or assisted in two tackles, and when a Concordia player fumbled the ball, David fell on it. As he held the recovered ball high, the crowd roared. It was an unforgettable moment for Augsburg fans!

David Lee Stevens was born to a woman who had taken thalidomide, an anti-nausea drug given to many pregnant women in the early sixties that was quickly proven to cause severe birth defects. David's feet appeared where his legs should have started. Abandoned by his mother, David was adopted by a foster family. Bee and Bill Stevens imposed strict rules of behavior on David, nurtured him, and loved him. They insisted he learn to do things for himself, and they never put him in a wheelchair. At age three, he was fitted with "legs."

In school, David became a student leader, made good grades, organized special events, and befriended new students. In high school, he played not only football but baseball, basketball, and hockey. He became a champion wrestler. When offered handicap license plates, he refused them, stating simply, "Those are for people who need them. I am not 'disabled.'"

David was taught to discipline himself, and so he was able to perform, in spite of his apparent handicap. Whatever obstacle may be in your way, self-discipline can help you either rise above it or plow right through it.

I keep **working** over **my body**.
I make it **obey me**.

1 CORINTHIANS 9:27 NLV

LET YOUR ACTIONS REFLECT YOUR BELIEFS

DURING THE KOREAN WAR, a South Korean civilian was arrested by the communists and sentenced to execution. When the young communist leader learned that the prisoner in his charge was the head of an orphanage caring for young children, he decided to spare him, but ordered that the man's son be executed in his place. The nineteen-year-old boy was shot in the presence of his father.

After the war, the United Nations captured the young communist leader. He was tried for his war crimes and condemned to death. Before the sentence could be carried out, however, the Christian whose son had been killed pleaded for the life of the killer. He argued that the communist had been young when he ordered the execution and that he really didn't know what he was doing. "Give him to me," the man requested, "and I will train him."

The United Nations forces granted the unusual request, and the father took the murderer of his son into his own home and cared for him. The young communist eventually became a Christian pastor.

For good or for bad, what we do speaks loudly. How vital it is that we do what we say!

> **WHAT YOU** do speaks so loud that I cannot hear what you say.
>
> Ralph Waldo Emerson

Show me your faith without deeds, and I will show you my faith by what I do.

JAMES 2:18 NIV

I hear people say "I love you" all the time. They love their favorite movie star. They love their favorite recording artist. They love pizza. Then every once in a while I hear someone say, "I love God." How can that word apply to all those things?

Love is an interesting word. Consider this. The Greeks have four words for love: Eros (romantic love), Stergo (affection between parents and children and other things, like masters for their dogs), Phila (friendship), and Agape (divine, unconditional love). In the Hebrew language, there are three words for love: Ahab (spontaneous, impulsive love), Hesed (deliberate affection and kindness), Raham (compassion and brotherly love). Fortunately for you, English has only one word, which is expressed in many different ways. It is a word that holds an infinite amount of emotion. Use it wisely. And it might be interesting to introduce some of these Greek and Hebrew words to your friends.

booklist

read all about it . . . goal-setting

- *Setting Godly Goals*
  by Dr. Charles Stanley

- *Balancing Your Life: Setting Personal Goals*
  by Paul Stevens

- *Setting Goals that Count: A Christian Perspective*
  by Joseph D. Allison

- *Checklist for Life for Teens*
  by Thomas Nelson Publishers

CONTINUE SETTING GOALS

After falling twice in the 1988 Olympic speed-skating races, Dan Jansen sought out sports psychologist Dr. Jim Loehr, who helped him find a new balance between sport and life, and who helped him pay more attention to the mental aspects of skating. Peter Mueller became his coach, putting him through workouts that Dan has since described as the "toughest I've ever known." By the time the 1994 Olympics arrived, Jansen had more confidence than ever. He had set a five-hundred-meter world record just two months before. That race seemed to be all his!

During the five-hundred-meter race, Jansen fell. He was shaken. Dr. Loehr immediately advised, "Start preparing for the one thousand. Put the five hundred behind you immediately. Stop reliving it." The one thousand! For years Dan had felt he could not win at that distance. He had always considered it his weaker event. Now it was his last chance for an Olympic medal. "As the race began," Jansen said, "I just seemed to be sailing along," and then he slipped and came within an inch of stepping on a lane marker. Still, he didn't panic. He raced on and recorded a world-record time that won him the gold medal!

Once you reach a goal or master a skill, set your sights higher. As you approach each goal, set a new one. Don't be intimidated! Your toughest goal can become your greatest triumph.

> **Unless** you try to do something beyond what you have already mastered, you will never grow.
> — Ronald E. Osborn

Straining **forward** to what lies **ahead,** I press on **toward** the goal for the prize of the **upward** call of God in **Christ Jesus.**

PHILIPPIANS 3:13-14 RSV

CONSIDER THIS!

Think about this way of spelling "A Pure Mind."

Acknowledge your vulnerability to God.

Pray for God's help.

Undo old thought processes.

Restrict what you view.

Eclipse bad thoughts with good thoughts.

Make yourself accountable to a Christian friend.

Imagine yourself resisting temptation.

Never despair when you fail. Keep trying.

Don't entertain impure thoughts that pop into your mind.

KEEP YOUR MIND PURE

According to an old legend, two monks named Tanzan and Ekido were traveling together down a muddy road one day. Heavy monsoon rains had saturated the area, and they were grateful for a few moments of sunshine to make their journey. Before long, they came around a bend and encountered a lovely girl in a silk kimono. She looked extremely forlorn as she stared at the muddy road before her.

At once, Tanzan responded to her plight. "Come here, girl," he said. Then lifting her in his arms, he carried her over the slippery ooze and set her down on the other side of the road.

Ekido didn't speak again to Tanzan. It was apparent to Tanzan that something was bothering him

> A WELL-TRAINED MEMORY IS ONE THAT PERMITS YOU TO FORGET EVERYTHING THAT ISN'T WORTH REMEMBERING.
>
> ORLANDO A. BATTISTA

deeply, but try as he would, he couldn't get Ekido to talk to him. Then that night after they reached their intended lodging, Ekido could no longer restrain his anger and disappointment. "We monks don't go near females," he said to Tanzan in an accusing voice. "We especially don't go near young and lovely maidens. It is dangerous. Why did you do that?"

"I left the girl back there, Ekido," replied Tanzan. Then he asked the key question, "Are you still carrying her?"

Train your mind to think on pure things. Make a conscious decision to stop any thought that doesn't line up with the teachings of the Bible. Take those thoughts captive! (See 2 Corinthians 10:5.)

Whatever is true, whatever is honorable, whatever is just . . . if there is any excellence, if there is anything worthy of praise, think about these things.

PHILIPPIANS 4:8 RSV

DO YOUR PART
TO OVERCOME

> **NO PLAN IS WORTH THE PAPER IT IS PRINTED ON UNLESS IT STARTS YOU DOING SOMETHING.**
>
> WILLIAM H. DANFORTH

NELSON DIEBEL, a hyperactive and delinquent child, was enrolled in The Peddie School where he met swimming coach, Chris Martin, who believed the more one practices, the better one performs. Within a month, he had Nelson swimming thirty to forty hours a week, even though Nelson could not sit still in a classroom for fifteen minutes. Martin saw potential in Nelson. He constantly put new goals in front of the boy, trying to get him to focus and turn his anger into strength. Nelson eventually qualified for the Junior Nationals, and his fast times qualified him for Olympic Trials.

Then Nelson broke both hands and arms in a diving accident, and doctors warned he probably would never regain his winning form. Martin said to him, "You're coming all the way back. . . . If you're not committed to that, we're going to stop right now." Nelson agreed, and within weeks after his casts were off, he was swimming again.

In 1992, Nelson Diebel won an Olympic gold medal. As he accepted his medal, he recalls thinking: *I planned and dreamed and worked so hard, and I did it!* The kid who once couldn't sit still and who had no ambition had learned to make a plan, pursue it, and achieve it. He had become a winner in far more than swimming!

Let your plans motivate you to start working toward your goals. Dream big dreams!

Be doers of the word, and not hearers only, deceiving yourselves.

JAMES 1:22 NKJV

TOP **10** TIPS for Creating a Plan to Achieve Your Goals

1. BRING GOD INTO YOUR PLANS. ASK FOR HIS HELP EACH DAY.

2. WRITE DOWN YOUR SPECIFIC GOALS.

3. LIST IN DETAIL THE STEPS NECESSARY TO ACCOMPLISH THOSE GOALS.

4. SCHEDULE THOSE STEPS INTO YOUR LIFE.

5. REVIEW YOUR PROGRESS EACH WEEK.

6. ASK FOR ADVICE FROM SOMEONE WHO HAS SUCCEEDED IN THE AREA IN WHICH YOU HOPE TO SUCCEED.

7. SEEK A MENTOR.

8. READ BOOKS THAT WILL EDUCATE YOU ABOUT HOW TO ACHIEVE YOUR GOALS.

9. OFFER TO DO AN INTERNSHIP.

10. RECORD YOUR ACCOMPLISHMENTS AND FAILURES. BOTH LEAD TO SUCCESS.

The memory of the
RIGHTEOUS
will be a blessing.

PROVERBS 10:7 NIV

> When you were born, you cried and the world rejoiced. Live your life in such a manner that when you die the world cries and you rejoice.

WHAT MEMORIES ARE YOU LEAVING?

A PAINTING IN AN ANCIENT temple depicts a king forging a chain from his crown, and nearby, another scene shows a slave converting his chain into a crown. Underneath the painting is this inscription: "Life is what one makes it, no matter of what it is made."

You may have been born with certain ingredients, just as a baker may find the staples of flour, sugar, and oil in his kitchen; but what you create from the talents and abilities God has given you is up to you! Live your life so that it might be measured according to these words of an anonymous poet:

Not—How did he die?
But—How did he live?
Not—What did he gain?
But—What did he give?
These are the units to measure
the worth
Of a man as a man,
regardless of birth.
Not—What was his station?
But—had he a heart?
And—How did he play his God-
given part?
Was he ever ready with a word of
good cheer,
To bring back a smile, to
banish a tear?
Not—What was his shrine?
Nor—What was his creed?
But—Had he befriended those
really in need?
Not—What did the sketch in
the newspaper say?
But—How many were sorry
when he passed away?

Who's Who:

Jonathan Grass

If you search the Web using the word "legacy," you will find an article published in the *Salisbury Post*, written by Jillian McCartney. The article is a tribute to the life of Jonathan Gross, who fought a rare form of bone cancer for two years and subsequently died at 22 years old. It seems that Jonathan left quite an impression on those around him.

"Jonathan never joined the military, but he was in God's army, and he was a good soldier. . . . He fought a good fight, and he did us proud," said his father.

Others had these words to say about Jonathan:

"His faith was unshakable."

"I'll always remember Jonathan as a guy who just gave."

"The key for him was that he always knew where he was going."

"[He} put others before himself."

"When you get to know him, it's like he's been a friend forever."

"He was faithful in the darkest hours...always looking to the future. It was 22 quality years."

In an e-mail shortly before his death, Jonathan wrote: "I know that the power of prayer and the healing hand of God have gotten me through this."

LET YOUR WORK REFLECT WHO YOU ARE

A young man once made an appointment with a well-published author. The first question the author asked him was, "Why did you want to see me?"

The young man stammered, "Well, I'm a writer too. I was hoping you could share with me some of your secrets for successful writing."

The author asked a second question, "What have you written?"

"Nothing," the young man replied, "at least nothing that is finished yet."

The author asked a third question, "Well, if you haven't written, then tell me, what are you writing?"

The young man replied, "Well, I'm in school right now, so I'm not writing anything at present."

The author then asked a fourth question, "So why do you call yourself a writer?"

Writers write. Composers compose. Painters paint. Workmen work. What you do to a great extent defines who you are and what you become. What does your work say about you? When your work on the outside coincides with who you are on the inside, you have found your true purpose in life and will find ultimate fulfillment.

> EVERY MAN'S WORK, WHETHER IT BE LITERATURE, OR MUSIC, OR PICTURES, OR ARCHITECTURE, OR ANYTHING ELSE, IS ALWAYS A PORTRAIT OF HIMSELF.
>
> SAMUEL BUTLER

AS IN WATER FACE REFLECTS FACE, SO THE HEART OF MAN REFLECTS MAN.

PROVERBS 27:19 NASB

WISE WORDS

Work is not primarily a thing one does to live, but the thing one lives to do. It is, or should be, the full expression of the worker's faculties, and the thing in which he finds spiritual, mental, and bodily satisfaction, and the medium in which he offers himself to God.

DOROTHY LEIGH SAYERS

DON'T LET EXCUSES SLOW YOU DOWN

SADIE DELANEY'S FATHER taught her always to strive to do better than her competition. She proved the value of that lesson shortly before she received her teaching license. A supervisor came to watch her and two other student teachers. Their assignment was to teach a class to bake cookies. Since the supervisor didn't have time for each teacher to go through the entire lesson, she divided the lesson, and Sadie was assigned to teach the girls how to serve and clean up.

The first student teacher panicked and forgot to halve the recipe and preheat the oven. The second girl was so behind because of the first girl's errors that the students made a mess in forming and baking the cookies. Then it was Sadie's turn. She said to the girls, "Listen, we have to work together as a team." They quickly baked the remaining dough. Several girls were lined up to scrub pans as soon as the cookies came out of the oven. Within ten minutes, they had several dozen perfect cookies and a clean kitchen.

The supervisor was so impressed, she offered Sadie a substitute teacher's license on the spot. Sadie soon became the first black person ever to teach domestic science in New York City's public high schools.

Even when you have every right to blame others who have gone before you, don't make excuses. Do what it takes to get the job done!

lighten up

Notes (allegedly from parents) collected by schools from all over the country:

- Please excuse Lisa for being absent. She was sick, and I had her shot.
- Dear School: Please ekscuse John being absent on Sept. 28, 29, 30, 31, 32, and also 33.
- Carlos was absent yesterday because he was playing football. He was hurt in the growing part.
- Please excuse Ray Friday from school. He has very loose vowels.

No discipline seems pleasant at the time, but vest of righteousness and peace for those who

> "Failures want pleasing methods, successes want pleasing results."
>
> EARL NIGHTINGALE

painful. Later on, however, it produces a har-
have been trained by it. HEBREWS 12:11 NIV

Facts

Which Old Testament prophet asked a poor widow to make him a meal with her very last provisions during a period of famine and drought?

The answer can be found in 1 Kings 17:9-16. God told Elijah to go immediately to Zarephath, where a widow would feed him. When Elijah reached the town gate, he saw a woman gathering sticks for her fire. He asked her for a drink of water and a piece of bread. She told him that she didn't have any bread, just a handful of flour in a jar and a little oil in a jug. "I am gathering sticks to go home and make a meal for me and my son," she told him, "so we can eat it, and then we'll die."

Elijah told her not to be afraid, but to go home and make that meal. But first she was to make a small cake for him from her provisions. Then he told her that the God of Israel says, "The jar of flour will not be used up and the jug of oil will not run dry until the day the Lord gives rain on the land." The widow did just what Elijah told her to do, and the miracle happened just as God had promised. Her jar of oil and jug of flour did not run out.

BE WISE WITH YOUR SEED

One of life's **great rules** is this:
The **more** you **give**,
the **more** you **get**.

William H. Danforth

Three young men were each given three kernels of corn by a wise old sage, who admonished them to go out into the world and use the corn to bring themselves good fortune.

The first young man put his three kernels of corn into a bowl of hot broth and ate them. The second thought, *I can do better than that*, and he planted his three kernels of corn. Within a few months, he had three stalks of corn. He took the ears of corn from the stalks, boiled them, and had enough corn for three meals.

The third man said to himself, *I can do better than that!* He also planted his three kernels of corn; but when his three stalks of corn produced, he stripped one of the ears and replanted all of the seeds in it, gave the second ear of corn to a sweet maiden, and ate the third. His one full ear's worth of replanted corn kernels gave him two hundred stalks of corn! The kernels of these he continued to replant, setting aside only a bare minimum to eat. He eventually planted a hundred acres of corn. With his fortune, he not only won the hand of the sweet maiden but also purchased the land owned by the sweet maiden's father. He never hungered again.

If you want to receive in life, you must first learn to give.

A liberal man will be
enriched, and one who waters
will himself be watered.

PROVERBS 11:25 RSV

CONSIDER ADVICE

After arguing heatedly for several hours about which type of water main to purchase for their city, the town council of Pacific Vista was still deadlocked. One member suggested, "Let's appoint a committee to confer with the city engineer at Los Angeles to find out which type they have found to be most successful over the years. If we can profit by another city's mistakes, I think we should do so."

> **Pride only** breeds quarrels, but wisdom is found in those who take advice.
>
> PROVERBS 13:10 NIV

Leaping to his feet, an angry councilman—obviously full of civic pride but with little discretion—replied, pounding his fist on the table, "Why should we have to profit by the mistakes of Los Angeles? Gentlemen, I contend that Pacific Vista is a big enough town now to make its own mistakes!"

Most of us are surrounded by good advice at any given time. The books in our libraries are full of it. Pastors proclaim it weekly. People with highly varied experiences and backgrounds abound with it. Schools give access to it; labs report it. Commentators and columnists gush with it. All the good advice in the world is worth very little if it is ignored. Be one of the wise—value and apply the advice you receive.

The way of a fool seems right to him,
but a wise man listens to advice.

PROVERBS 12:15 NIV

✓ JUST DO IT

#1   **Try these ideas for collecting and using words of wisdom and sound advice:**

1. Carry a small spiral notebook or index cards in your pocket or backpack to write down words of wisdom.
2. Pay close attention to advice given by older, trusted people in your circle.
3. Interview your grandparents. You won't believe the words of wisdom and sound advice you will receive.
4. E-mail your pastor and ask him to share with you a few words from the Lord.
5. Make a list of five ways you can apply to everyday life the advice you've collected.

CONSIDER
THIS!

These are just a few of the promises God has made to believers:

A crown of life	Revelation 2:10
A heavenly home	John 14:1-3
A new name	Isaiah 62:1-2
Answers to prayer	1 John 5:14
Assurance	2 Timothy 1:12
Cleansing	John 15:3
Clothing	Zechariah 3:4
Comfort	Isaiah 51:3
Companionship	John 15:15
Fellowship of Jesus	Matthew 18:19
God's protecting care	1 Peter 5:6-7
Growth	Ephesians 4:11-15
Guidance	Isaiah 42:16
Hope	Hebrews 6:18-19
Inheritance	1 Peter 1:3-4
Joy	Isaiah 35:10
Knowledge	Jeremiah 24:7
Liberty	Romans 8:2
Peace	John 14:27
Renewal	Titus 3:5
Rest	Hebrews 4:9,11
Spiritual healing	Hosea 6:1
Strength	Philippians 4:13
Temporal blessings	Matthew 6:25-33
Understanding	Psalm 119:104
Wisdom	James 1:5

FAITH ON THE INSIDE, WORKS ON THE OUTSIDE

Wallace E. Johnson, president of Holiday Inns and one of America's most successful builders, once said, "I always keep a card in my billfold with the following verses and refer to them frequently: 'Ask, and it shall be given you; seek, and ye shall find; knock, and it shall be opened unto you: for every one that asketh receiveth; and he that seeketh findeth; and to him that knocketh it shall be opened' (Matthew 7:7-8).

THE SECRET OF SUCCESS IS TO BE LIKE A DUCK– SMOOTH AND UNRUFFLED ON TOP, BUT PADDLING FURIOUSLY UNDERNEATH.

"These verses are among God's greatest promises. Yet they are a little one-sided. They indicate a philosophy of receiving but not of giving. One day as my wife, Alma, and I were seeking God's guidance for a personal problem, I came across the following verse which has since been a daily reminder to me of what my responsibility as a businessman is to God: 'Study to shew thyself approved unto God, a workman that needeth not to be ashamed, rightly dividing the word of truth' (2 Timothy 2:15).

"Since then I have measured my actions against the phrase: A workman that needeth not to be ashamed."

Faith on the inside—works on the outside—a successful life!

Haven't I worked hard trying to do more than any of the others? Even then, my work didn't amount to all that much. It was God giving me the work to do, God giving me the energy to do it.

1 CORINTHIANS 15:10 MSG

THERE IS POWER IN OVERCOMING LUST

THE WORLD WANTS YOUR BEST, BUT GOD WANTS YOUR ALL.

IN *THE GREAT Divorce*, C.S. Lewis tells the story of a ghost who carries a little red lizard on his shoulder. The lizard constantly twitches its tail and whispers to the ghost, who all the while urges it to be quiet. When a bright and shining presence appears and offers to rid the ghost of his troublesome baggage, the ghost refuses. He realizes that to quiet the beast, it is necessary to kill it.

A series of rationalizations begins. The ghost reasons that perhaps the lizard need not die but instead might be trained, suppressed, put to sleep, or gradually removed. The shining presence responds that the only recourse is all or nothing.

Finally, the ghost gives permission for the presence to twist the lizard away from him. The presence breaks the lizard's back as he flings it to the ground. In that moment, the ghost becomes a flesh-and-blood man, and the lizard becomes a beautiful gold-and-silver stallion, a creature of power and beauty. The man leaps onto the great horse, and they ride into the sunrise as one.

Lewis concludes by saying, "What is a lizard compared with a stallion? Lust is a poor, weak, whimpering, whispering thing compared with that richness and energy of desire which will arise when lust has been killed."

Jesus said to him, "You must love the Lord your God with all your heart, all your soul, and all your mind."

MATTHEW 22:37 NLT

TOP 10 TIPS for Improving Your Lust–Busting Skills

1. ASK GOD FOR A PURE MIND.

2. BE CAREFUL WHAT YOU WATCH ON TELEVISION OR AT THE MOVIES.

3. MEMORIZE SCRIPTURE AND QUOTE IT WHENEVER YOU FEEL WEAK AND VULNERABLE.

4. REMEMBER THAT YOU HAVE THE ABILITY TO DEFEND YOUR MIND AGAINST EVIL THOUGHTS.

5. AVOID SITUATIONS WHERE YOU HAVE BEEN TEMPTED IN THE PAST.

6. READ ONLY CHRISTIAN BOOKS AND MAGAZINES.

7. SAY NO TO FRIENDS WHO ENTICE YOU INTO QUESTIONABLE ACTIVITIES.

8. SAY YES TO FRIENDS WHO WILL HELP YOU AVOID TEMPTATION.

9. INSTALL CHILD CONTROLS ON YOUR COMPUTER TO AVOID UNWELCOME POP-UPS AND TO HELP YOU STAY AWAY FROM INAPPROPRIATE SITES.

10. REMEMBER THAT THE BATTLE IS THE LORD'S. CALL UPON HIS MERCY AND GRACE.

fyi booklist

read more about it. . . pleasing god

- *Pleasing God*
  by R. C. Sproul

- *The Practice of the Presence of God*
  by Brother Lawrence

- *Pleasing God: 9 Studies for Individuals or Groups*
  by Jack Kuhatschek

- *Finding God*
  by Larry Crabb

- *Surrendering Your Life for God's Pleasure*
  by Brett Eastman

YOU NEED ONLY PLEASE ONE

A young man once studied violin under a world-renowned violinist and master teacher. He worked hard for several years at perfecting his talent, and the day finally came when he was called upon to give his first major public recital in the large city where both he and his teacher lived. Following each selection, which he performed with great skill and passion, the performer seemed uneasy about the great applause he received. Even though he knew that those in the audience were musically astute and not likely to give such applause to a less than superior performance, the young man acted almost as if he couldn't hear the appreciation that was being showered upon him.

> **I don't know** the secret to success, but the key to failure is to try to please everyone.
>
> Bill Cosby

At the close of the last number, the applause was thunderous and numerous "Bravos" were shouted, but the talented young violinist had his eyes glued on one spot only. Finally, when an elderly man in the first row of the balcony smiled and nodded to him in approval, the young man relaxed and beamed with both relief and joy. His teacher had praised his work! The applause of thousands meant nothing until he had first won the approval of the master.

Who are you trying to please today? You will never be able to please everyone, but you can please the One who matters most—your Father God. Keep your eyes on Him, and you can't fail.

Am I now trying to win the approval of men, or of God?

GALATIANS 1:10 NIV

HOW Do YOU MEASURE Up?

Surveys reveal that many Christians believe that it is okay to break the rules or be dishonest when circumstances warrant. If that is true, what makes believers different from unbelievers? Provide yes or no answers to the following questions.

I think it is okay under certain circumstances to:
A. Tell a lie.
B. Steal.
C. Swear.
D. Strike someone.
E. Gossip.
F. Have sex before marriage.
G. Cheat on a test.
H. Break a traffic law.

Now, read through the book of Proverbs and see what God thinks about these specific issues.

LET YOUR DEEDS REFLECT YOUR INTEGRITY

OUR DEEDS DE-TERMINE US, AS MUCH AS WE DETERMINE OUR DEEDS.

GEORGE ELLIOT

In the fourth round of a national spelling bee in Washington, eleven-year-old Rosalie Elliot, a champion from South Carolina, was asked to spell the word avowal. Her soft Southern accent made it difficult for the judges to determine if she had used an "a" or an "e" as the next-to-last letter of the word. They deliberated for several minutes and also listened to tape-recorded playbacks, but they still couldn't determine which letter had been pronounced. Finally the chief judge, John Lloyd, put the question to the only person who knew the answer. He asked Rosalie, "Was the letter an a or an e?"

Rosalie, surrounded by whispering young spellers, knew by now the correct spelling of the word; but without hesitation, she replied that she had misspelled the word and had used an e.

As she walked from the stage, the entire autience—including dozens of newspaper reporters covering the event—stood and applauded her honesty and integrity. While Rosalie had not won the contest, she had definitely come out a winner that day.

We often think that who we are determines what we do. Equally true, what you do today will determine, in part, who you become tomorrow.

Even a **child** is known by his **actions,** by whether his **conduct** is **pure** and **right.**

PROVERBS 20:11 NIV

ONLY SPEAK GOOD WORDS

A man once sat down to have dinner with his family. Before they began to eat, the family members joined hands around the table, and the man said a prayer, thanking God for the food, the hands that had prepared it, and for the source of all life. During the meal, however, he complained at length about the staleness of the bread, the bitterness of the coffee, and a bit of mold he found on one edge of the brick of cheese.

His young daughter asked him, "Daddy, do you think God heard you say grace before the meal?"

"Of course, honey," he answered confidently.

Then she asked, "Do you think God heard everything that was said during dinner?" The man answered, "Why, yes, I believe so. God hears everything."

She thought for a moment and then asked, "Daddy, which do you think God believed?"

The Lord hears everything we say during a day, not only those words that are addressed specifically to Him. Once you've said something, you can't take it back. Would you mind if God listened in on your conversations?

> ONCE A WORD HAS BEEN ALLOWED TO ESCAPE, IT CANNOT BE RECALLED.
>
> HORACE

DON'T USE FOUL OR ABUSIVE LANGUAGE. LET EVERYTHING YOU SAY BE GOOD AND HELPFUL, SO THAT YOUR WORDS WILL BE AN ENCOURAGEMENT TO THOSE WHO HEAR THEM.

EPHESIANS 4:29 NLT

WISE WORDS

Cold words freeze people, and hot words scorch them, and bitter words make them bitter, and wrathful words make them wrathful. Kind words also produce their image on men's souls; and a beautiful image it is. They smooth, and quiet, and comfort the hearer.

BLAISE PASCAL

In a race everyone runs but only one person gets

FIRST PRIZE.

. . . To win the contest you must deny yourselves many things that would keep you from

doing your best.

1 CORINTHIANS 9:24-25 TLB

NO EXCUSES

CHARLES OAKLEY, FORWARD for the New York Knicks and an NBA All-Star, has a reputation for being one of basketball's best rebounders. It's his toughness, however, that has probably contributed the most to his outstanding sports career.

While other professional players seem to have frequent injuries or are sidelined for other reasons, Oakley has had very few injuries over the course of his thirteen-year career, even though he has absorbed a great deal of physical punishment on the court. He is often pushed and fouled. He puts in miles each game running up and down the court. He frequently dives into the stands for loose balls, to the extent that the courtside media teases him about being a working hazard. According to Oakley, his tenacity and energy have an origin: his grandfather, Julius Moss.

Moss was a farmer in Alabama who did most of his fieldwork by hand. "Other people had more equipment than he did," Oakley says. "He didn't have a tractor, but he got the work done. No excuses." Moss, who died in 1990, developed all sorts of aches and pains in his life, but he laughed at them and went about his business. Oakley saw a lesson in that—nothing should prevent him from earning a day's pay.

Being focused, dedicated, and disciplined will make the difference between a mediocre life and a great life.

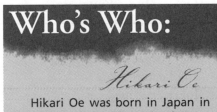

Who's Who:

Hikari Oe was born in Japan in 1963 with what appeared to be two heads. Doctors encouraged his parents to let the boy die and forget about him. They predicted he would never be more than a vegetable, but his parents refused. They opted for a highly risky operation, which Hikari somehow survived, but it left him epileptic, developmentally delayed (an IQ of 65), visually impaired, and with limited physical coordination.

When he was sixteen, the boy spoke his first word. By 32, Hikari still spoke only a few words, but he had learned to express himself through a different venue—Hikari has become an award-winning classical Japanese composer. Not bad for a "vegetable."

Hikari made no excuses and did not settle for a mediocre life.

YOUR FUTURE IS SPOTLESS

WILLINGWAY HOSPITAL is one of the nation's top treatment centers for alcoholism and drug addiction. There would be no Willingway, however, if it weren't for Dot and John, who at one time seemed the least likely candidates to found such a hospital. Early in their courtship, Dot and John drank heavily, and after they married, they began taking amphetamines. John, a medical doctor, was arrested for writing himself narcotics prescriptions. He spent six months in prison, eventually falling on his knees and crying out to God for help in overcoming his addictions.

When John returned to medical practice drug free and alcohol free, he began to receive referrals from other doctors to treat their alcoholic patients. Dot and John set up three beds under the chandelier in their own dining room as a detox room. Among their patients have been three of their own four children, each of whom struggled with addictions.

As word of their compassion spread, they established a forty-bed hospital on eleven acres close to their home. The chandelier still hangs in the detox room as a symbol of hope. All four children have worked on the medical staff or administration of Willingway. With God's help, they truly became a family in full recovery.

Regardless of our past, the future is a blank slate, waiting to be written upon.

> **No Matter** what a man's past may have been, his future is spotless.
>
> JOHN R. RICE

No, dear brothers and sisters, I am still not all I should be, but I am focusing all my energies on this one thing: Forgetting the past and looking forward to what lies ahead.

PHILIPPIANS 3:13 NLT

new insights into ageless questions

Everyone tells me that God is loving and kind. If He is, why is there so much pain in the world? Why doesn't God come to the rescue of those who are suffering?

Many books have been written that speculate on why bad things happen to people, why there is so much pain and suffering even for those who believe in God. It's a question with an answer as big as God himself. Here it is in a nutshell. The Bible says that in the perfect world He created for us, there was no pain or suffering. The problem is that God gave men and women a free will, and their actions allowed sin and suffering to enter the world. Imagine that your parents gave you food and clothing, but you decided to throw it away. Then, cold and hungry, you accused them of not caring about you. Humankind has put itself in this pickle. And yet, God has not abandoned us.

In Romans 8:28 Paul writes that all things work together for good in the lives of those who love the Lord. God does not promise us that we will never suffer or experience pain. Life is full of tough circumstances and painful events. But He does promise to stay with us, hold our hands during the bad times, and when it is over, redeem our suffering by causing something good to come out of it.

CONSIDER
THIS!

The mass of men lead lives of quiet desperation. What is called resignation is confirmed desperation. From the desperate city you go into the desperate country and have to console yourself with the bravery of minks and muskrats. A stereotyped but unconscious despair is concealed even under what are called the games and amusements of mankind. There is no play in them, for this comes after work. But it is a characteristic of wisdom not to do desperate things.

When we consider what, to use the words of the catechism, is the chief end of man, and what are the true necessaries and means of life, it appears as if men had deliberately chosen the common mode of living because they preferred it to any other. Yet they honestly think there is no choice left. But alert and healthy natures remember that the sun rose clear. It is never too late to give up our prejudices.

HENRY DAVID THOREAU

WORTHWHILE INVESTMENTS

Frank, the head and founder of a major contracting firm, refused to celebrate the holidays, saying only, "Christmas is for children." Then one brisk December day, Frank was walking to work and was drawn to a Nativity scene in a department store window. He saw the Child anew. As he started to move away, a sign across the street caught his attention: "Holy Innocents Home." His mind raced back to a Sunday school lesson he had heard years ago about how King Herod had feared the baby Jesus and slaughtered children in Bethlehem. He recalled the day his own son, David, had died at the age of eighteen months. He had not been able to speak his name since.

Impulsively, Frank visited the library and was surprised to learn that Herod's men were estimated to have killed twenty children. He left the library with a mission. Later that night, he told his wife, Adele, that he had visited the orphanage and that he had given money for the building of a new wing. Then he said, "They are going to name it for David." What Frank did not tell his wife was that he had had a vision of twenty children playing in a bright new wing at Holy Innocents. As Adele hugged him, the vision came again, but this time, there were twenty-one children at play.

Don't miss the opportunity to spend your life on something worthwhile. You may have several opportunities, some big and some small, but none of them will be insignificant.

LIFE IS A COIN. YOU CAN SPEND IT ANY WAY YOU WISH, BUT YOU CAN SPEND IT ONLY ONCE.

LILLIAN DICKSON

It is appointed for men to die once, but after this the judgment.

HEBREWS 9:27 NKJV

WINNING FRIENDS

Mary Lennox "was not an affectionate child and had never cared much for anyone"; and no wonder. Ignored by her parents and raised by servants, she had no concept of what life was like outside of India. Other children called her "Mistress Mary Quite Contrary," because she didn't like to share and always insisted on having her own way.

THE ONLY WAY TO HAVE A FRIEND IS TO BE ONE.

RALPH WALDO EMERSON

When Mary was nine years old, her parents died of cholera, and she was sent to live at her uncle's home in England. The move did nothing to improve her disposition. She expected anyone and everyone to jump when she snapped her fingers.

Gradually, however, Mary began to change. Realizing how lonely she was, she asked a robin in the garden to be her friend. She began treating her maid with more respect. Won over by the guilelessness of her maid's little brother, Dickon, and craving his approval, Mary found herself seeking his advice. She even revealed to him the location of her secret garden.

Eventually, Mary convinced her crippled cousin, Colin, to grab hold of life with both hands. By the last page of *The Secret Garden*, Mary's transformation is complete. She is happy with herself and surrounded by friends.

To make a friend, you first must make a choice to become a friend.

A MAN WHO HAS FRIENDS MUST HIMSELF BE FRIENDLY.

PROVERBS 18:24 NKJV

The world is so empty if one thinks only of mountains, rivers, and cities; but to know someone here and there who thinks and feels with us, and who, though distant, is close to us in spirit, this makes the earth an inhabited garden.

GOETHE

THE NECESSARY BUSINESS OF CONFRONTATION

IN *LIFE'S BOTTOM LINE,* Richard Exley writes, "Several weeks ago I was agonizing over a situation in which I had to discipline a man. Though I felt I had done the right thing, and in the right way, I still grieved for him. As I was wrestling with my feelings in prayer, I sensed the Lord speaking to me, and I wrote: "My son, power is a dangerous thing, and it must always be mitigated with My eternal love. I will cause you to feel the pain of My discipline even when it is toward another. You will feel every sting of the lash in your own flesh. You must, or in your zealousness you would go too far. You will grieve, even as Samuel grieved for Saul. Yet I will also make you feel the awful pain of their sin, for if you do not feel that terrible pain, you

will draw back from administering the discipline of the Lord."

Exley concludes, "Confrontation is invariably necessary. A relationship seldom achieves its full potential without it; but it is almost always doomed to failure unless it grows out of a deep trust built on honest communication. . . . It is extremely important to take great care to create a safe place of affirmation and acceptance, where a person can be assured, again and again, of our love. Even then, confrontation will be risky and should be undertaken only after we have carefully prepared our hearts before the Lord."

A true friend cares enough to tell you when you're going the wrong way. Don't be afraid to confront a friend, and be willing to listen when a friend confronts you. It's one reason God gave us friends—to help us grow.

lighten up

A teacher in a school where corporal punishment is forbidden sent this note to the mother of an unruly pupil: "Dear Mrs. Jones, I regret very much to inform you that your son, Robert, idles away his time, is disobedient and quarrelsome, and disturbs other students who are trying to work. He needs a good thrashing, and I strongly urge that you give him one."

This reply came back: "Dear Miss Smith, Lick him yourself. I ain't mad at him."

If one falls down, his friend can help him up. But pity

"A true friend never gets in your way unless you happen to be going down."

Arnold Glasgow

the man who falls and has no one to help him up!

booklist

read more about it...
the power of words

- *Healing Words for the Body, Mind and Spirit: 101 Words to Inspire and Affirm*
  by Caren Goldman, Belleruth Naparstek

- *The Power of Your Words*
  by Don Gossett, E. W. Kenyon

- *The Right Words at the Right Time*
  by Marlo Thomas

- *Words That Hurt, Words That Heal : How to Choose Words Wisely and Well*
  by Joseph Telushkin

DON'T DAMPEN ANOTHER'S ZEAL

IN THE 1700s AN ENGLISH cobbler kept a map of the world on his workshop wall so that he might be reminded to pray for the nations of the world. As the result of such prayer, he became especially burdened for a specific missionary outreach. He shared this burden at a meeting of ministers but was told by a senior minister, "Young man, sit down. When God wants to convert the heathen, He will do it without your help or mine."

The cobbler, William Carey, did not let this man's remarks put out the flame of his concern. When he couldn't find others to support the missionary cause that had burdened his soul, he became a missionary himself. His pioneering efforts in India are legendary; his mighty exploits for God are recorded by many church historians.

Be careful how you respond to the enthusiasm of others. Don't dampen someone's zeal for God. Be cautious in how you respond to the new ideas of another, that you don't squelch their God-given creativity.

Be generous and kind in evaluating the work of others so that you might encourage those things that are worthy. Be slow to judge and quick to praise. Then pray for the same in your own life!

> **Those** that have done nothing in life are not qualified to judge those that have done little.
> Samuel Johnson

"Judge not, and you shall not be judged. Condemn not, and you shall not be condemned."

LUKE 6:37 NKJV

Fun Facts

Question: Which of Edgar Allan Poe's poems is the most recognized today and what is the most famous line in the poem?

Hint: A motion picture was made around the premise of this poem.

Answer. "The Raven" was the name of the poem. The most famous line in the poem was: "Quoth the Raven, 'Nevermore'." Do you remember the film starring Vincent Price?

Question: When and where was Edgar Allen Poe born? And when and where did he die?

Answer: Edgar Allen Poe was born in Boston, January 19, 1809, and after a tempestuous life of forty years, he died in the city of Baltimore, October 7, 1849.

CIRCUMSTANCES CAN'T CONTROL YOUR OUTCOME

Defeat is not the **worst** of **failures**.
Not to have **tried** is the **true failure**.

George Edward Woodberry

There once was a young man who lived a most miserable life. Orphaned before he was three, he was taken in by strangers. He was kicked out of school, suffered from poverty, and as the result of inherited physical weaknesses, he developed serious heart trouble as a teenager. His beloved wife died early in their marriage. He lived as an invalid most of his adult life, and he eventually died at the young age of forty. By all outward appearances, he was defeated by life and doomed to be forgotten by history.

Even so, he never quit trying to express himself and to achieve success over the twenty years of his active work life. In that period, he produced some of the most brilliant articles, essays, and criticisms ever written. His poetry is still read widely and studied by virtually every high school student in the United States. His short stories and detective stories are famous. One of his poems, on display at the famous Huntington Library in California, has been valued at more than fifty thousand dollars, which is far more than the young man earned in his entire lifetime.

His name? Edgar Allan Poe.

Circumstances don't affect your chances for success nearly as much as your level of effort!

God said to Joshua, "Be strong and of good courage; be not frightened, neither be dismayed; for the Lord your God is with you wherever you go."

JOSHUA 1:9 RSV

SILENCE ISN'T ALWAYS GOLDEN

> THERE ARE TIMES WHEN SILENCE IS GOLDEN, OTHER TIMES IT IS JUST PLAIN YELLOW.
>
> ED COLE

ACCORDING to an old fable, three men once decided to engage in the religious practice of absolute silence. They mutually agreed to keep a day of quiet from dawn until the stroke of midnight, at which time a full moon was expected to rise from the horizon. They sat cross-legged for hours, concentrating on the distant horizon, eager for darkness to envelop them.

One of them unwittingly noted, "It's difficult not to say anything at all."

The second one replied, "Quiet. You're speaking during the time of silence!"

The third man sighed and then boasted, "Now I'm the only one who hasn't spoken yet."

A rap singer has updated some of the advice given by the book of Ecclesiastes:

There's a time to speak up and a time to shut up.

There's a time to hunker down and a time to go downtown.

There's a time to talk and a time to walk. There's a time to be mellow and a time not to be yellow.

Silence can be good, but never if it's the result of raw fear or lack of moral fiber.

There is an appointed time for everything. . . . a time to be silent and a time to speak.

ECCLESIASTES 3:1,7 NASB

TOP 10 TIPS for Learning When to Be Quiet

1. WHEN SOMEONE IS GRIEVING, OPT TO GIVE YOUR PRESENCE AND A HUG.

2. WHEN YOU ARE ANGRY.

3. WHEN YOU ARE TEMPTED TO GOSSIP.

4. WHEN YOU WANT TO CRITICIZE.

5. WHEN YOU ARE ABOUT TO LIE.

6. WHEN SOMEONE ELSE IS SPEAKING.

7. WHEN YOU'VE ALREADY SAID TOO MUCH.

8. WHEN WHAT YOU HAVE TO SAY WILL HURT INSTEAD OF HELP.

9. WHEN A FRIEND NEEDS YOU TO SIMPLY LISTEN.

10. WHEN YOU WANT TO ARGUE WITH YOUR PARENTS.

HOW Do YOU MEASURE Up?

It can be difficult to wait for something to happen or for a life-changing question to be answered. How do you respond when you are asked to wait for God's answer?

When God doesn't answer right away, I:
A. Go on with my life.
B. Get angry with God and pout.
C. Distract myself with friends and lots of activities?
D. Challenge myself with something new.
E. Do my best to trust God even though I may feel like a basket case.

God always answers our prayers. But sometimes the answer is "not yet." When God answers you in that way, He has a reason—one that is in your best interest. Pouting or getting angry serves no purpose and could actually keep you from receiving what you have asked God for. Trust Him to do what is best for you, and you will never be disappointed.

HUSTLE WHILE YOU WAIT

EVERYTHING COMES TO HIM WHO HUSTLES WHILE HE WAITS.

THOMAS A. EDISON

In 1928, a happy, ambitious young nursing student was diagnosed with tuberculosis. Her family sent her to a nursing home in Saranac Lake for several months of curing. She would remain in bed for twenty-one years! Most people may have given up, but not Isabel Smith. She approached the threshold of death on several occasions, but she never ceased to pursue the art of living. She read voraciously, loved to write letters, studied geography, and taught other patients to read and write. From her bed, she studied atomic energy with a fellow patient, a young physicist, and organized a town hall meeting on the topic.

While ill, she met a kind, gentle man, who was also a patient at the sanitarium. She dreamed of marrying him and having a little house "under the mountains." At her lowest ebb, her dream kept her going, and in 1948, they did marry. She then wrote a book about "all the good things life has brought me." *Wish I Might*, published in 1955, earned her enough in royalties to buy her mountain retreat.

A tragic life? Hardly! Isabel Smith achieved everything she set out to achieve, even when the odds against her were a thousand to one. Even flat on her back in bed, she never quit growing, learning, and giving.

We do not want you to become lazy, but to imitate those who through faith and patience inherit what has been promised. Hebrews

6:12 NIV

SHARING GOD'S LOVE

The story is told of a small dog that was struck by a car and tossed to the edge of the road. A doctor, who just happened to be driving by, noticed that the dog was still alive, so he stopped his car, picked up the dog, and took him home with him. He discovered the dog had suffered only a few minor cuts and abrasions. Reviving the dog, the doctor cleaned its wounds, then carried it to the garage, where he intended to provide a temporary bed.

"Go into the world. Go everywhere and announce the Message of God's good news to one and all."

MARK 16:15 MSG

The dog wriggled free from his arms, however, jumped to the ground, and scampered off. "What an ungrateful dog," the doctor said to himself. He was glad that the dog had recovered so quickly, but was a little miffed that the dog had shown so little appreciation for his expert, gentle care.

He thought no more about the incident until the next evening, when he heard a scratching at his front door. When he opened the door, he found the little dog he had treated. At its side was another injured dog!

Be encouraged! You may never see the difference you make in someone's life or the difference that person will make in the lives of others; nevertheless, those with whom you share the Gospel will never be the same.

The Gospel is neither a discussion nor a debate. It is an announcement.

PAUL S. REES

☑ JUST DO IT

#1 **It is within the context of a caring relationship that hearts open to hear the Gospel. Use the following tips to create a caring environment with lost souls.**

#2 1. Volunteer once a month at a shelter or mission.

2. Volunteer to be a big brother or sister to a child's family.

#3 3. Defend someone who is an outcast or is being bullied.

4. Befriend someone who is new to your school or neighborhood.

5. Offer to help a single-parent family.

#4

#5

#6

#7

#8

#9

#10

CONSIDER THIS!

In Matthew 7:24, Jesus told His disciples how to establish a firm foundation for a spiritual house—one that could withstand the storms of life. He told them to listen carefully to His words and then act upon them. Wise words and righteous actions form a bedrock that will allow your spiritual house to stand, undamaged, even when rain and floods and wind beat at it. Without this rock foundation, He cautioned them, they would soon find the wind and water rising and washing sand out from under them.

Does your spiritual life have a firm, bedrock foundation? If not, don't delay. Pick up your Bible and read a passage daily. Ask God to help you live out the truth in the words you are reading. He is eager to help you become established in every area of your life.

WORK AS IF FOR YOURSELF AND GOD

Joe Smith was a loyal carpenter who worked almost two decades for a successful contractor. The contractor called him into his office one day and said, "Joe, I'm putting you in charge of the next house we build. I want you to order all the materials and oversee the job from the ground up."

Joe accepted the assignment with great enthusiasm. He studied the blueprints and checked every measurement and specification. Suddenly he had a thought. *If I'm really in charge, why couldn't I cut a few corners, use less expensive materials, and put the extra money in my pocket? Who will know? Once the house is painted, it will look great.*

So Joe set about his scheme. He ordered second-grade lumber and inexpensive concrete, put in cheap wiring, and cut every corner he could. When the home was finished, the contractor came to see it.

"What a fine job you've done!" he said. "You've been such a faithful carpenter to me all these years that I've decided to show you my gratitude by giving you a gift—this house."

Build well today. You will have to live with the character and reputation you construct.

YOU ARE ONLY WHAT YOU ARE WHEN NO ONE IS LOOKING.

ROBERT C. EDWARD

Bondservants, be **obedient** . . . **Not** with *eyeservice*, as **men-pleasers**, but as **bondservants** of **Christ**, doing the **will** of **God** from the **heart**.

EPHESIANS 6:6 NKJV

PUT A LID ON IT

A young attorney, just out of law school and beginning his first day on the job, sat down in the comfort of his brand-new office with a great sigh of satisfaction.

He had worked long and hard to savor such a moment. Then, noticing a prospective client coming toward his door, he began to look busy and energetic. Opening his legal pad and uncapping his pen, he picked up the telephone, and cradling it under his chin, he began to write furiously as he said, "Look, Harry, about that amalgamation deal. I think I better run down to the factory and handle it personally. Yes. No. I don't think three million dollars will swing it. We better have Smith from Los Angeles meet us there. Okay. Call you back later."

Hanging up the phone, he put down his pen, looked up at his visitor, stood, extended his hand, and said in his most polite but confident attorney's voice, "Good morning. How might I help you?"

The prospective client replied, "Actually, I'm just here to hook up your phone."

Many a foible or flaw
Need not show . . . for
If you don't say so,
Others won't know!

There's an old saying that goes, "A shut mouth gathers no foot." Sometimes the best thing to do is just keep your mouth shut!

> I HAVE NEVER BEEN HURT BY ANYTHING I DIDN'T SAY.
>
> CALVIN COOLIDGE

DON'T TALK SO MUCH. YOU KEEP PUTTING YOUR FOOT IN YOUR MOUTH. BE SENSIBLE AND TURN OFF THE FLOW!

PROVERBS 10:19 TLB

WISE WORDS

We all have a deep inner need for some silence, to be silent ourselves, to enjoy silence itself; an increasing need in an ever-noisier world. Psychiatrists are trying to impress that fact upon us, to convince us of the virtues of silence and of its value in living fully today. We are . . . familiar with people beset with the urge to talk for talk's sake; most of us do just that far more often than we probably realize. . . . So we say something, when silence would be preferable—and wiser.

DAVID GUNSTON

"Seek and you will find; KNOCK and the door will be opened to you."

MATTHEW 7:7 NIV

KEEP YOUR EYES OPEN FOR OPPORTUNITIES

IN 1970, WALLY STARTED baking chocolate chip cookies for his friends, using a recipe and procedure that had been passed down from his Aunt Della. For five years, he gave away every batch he made, even though people often told him that his cookies were so good that he should go into business and sell them. Wally had other ideas though. He was determined to become a big-time show-business manager.

Then one day a friend, B.J. Gilmore, told him that she had a friend who could put up the money for a cookie-making business. Her friend never made the investment, but Wally got some of his own friends—including Jeff Wall, Helen Reddy, and Marvin Gaye—to put up some money. Then Wally was off and running.

Originally, he intended to open up only one store on Sunset Boulevard, just enough to make a living. After all, his was the only store in the world dedicated to the sale of nothing but chocolate chip cookies. Business grew virtually overnight. Wally's "Famous Amos Chocolate Chip Cookies" were soon distributed worldwide. Wally himself became a spokesman for other products, from eggs to airlines to a telephone company. While he once dreamed of managing stars, he now is one in his own right!

Sometimes dreams come through the back door. Keep it unlocked.

Who's Who:

Bessie Coleman

The tenth child in a sharecropper's family of thirteen children, Bessie Coleman was determined to "amount to something." There weren't many opportunities for a black girl in the south in the 1890s. But Bessie managed to finish all eight grades of school—all she was allowed at that time.

Bessie took every opportunity that came her way. She moved to Chicago to live with her brothers and attend beauty school. She was working as a manicurist at a beauty shop when her brothers told her that in France women could have careers—they could even fly airplanes!

Bessie applied at schools in the U.S., but was denied because she was a black woman. Undeterred, she took a course in French, saved the money she made working in a chili parlor, and then set out for France. On July 15, 1921, Bessie Coleman became the first black woman to be awarded a pilot's license. She eventually became an American show pilot, performing in flying exhibitions. No matter what obstacles she encountered, she refused to let it stop her. She watched for opportunities and when they came, she was ready!

A FRESH PERSPECTIVE

AFTER TWO YEARS IN THE navy, Willard Scott returned to his old job with NBC radio, but to a new supervisor. Willard found himself at odds with his new boss at every turn, and he was furious when he rescheduled Joy Boys, a comedy show Willard did with Eddie Walker, for the worst slot on radio—eight to midnight. Willard was braced for a change-or-I'll-leave confrontation when he recalled Proverbs 19:11 NIV—"A man's wisdom gives him patience; it is to his glory to overlook an offense." He and Eddie decided to work themselves to the bone, and within three years, they made Joy Boys the top-rated show in Washington.

Willard says, "I learned that I, too, had been wrong. In all my dealings with my boss, I had aggravated the problem. I knew he didn't like me, and in response I was barely civil to him and dodged him as much as I could; but one day he invited me to a station party I couldn't avoid. There I met his fiancée. She was bright, alive, and down-to-earth.

How could a woman like that care for anybody who didn't have something to recommend him? I was able to get new insight into my boss's character. As time went on my attitude changed, and so did his." Willard and his boss became friends, and he remained at NBC.

Is there someone with whom you are at odds? If you're looking for the negative qualities in a person, you're sure to find them. Try seeing them with new eyes. A fresh perspective can change everything.

lighten up

A change in perspective can happen when you least expect it. For instance, think about these brain teasers:

- If camels are called the ships of the desert, why aren't tugboats called the camels of the sea?

- If we call oranges oranges, why don't we call bananas yellows, or apples reds?

- What happens to your lap when you stand up?

> "Hating people is like burning down your own house to get rid of a rat."
>
> HARRY EMERSON FOSDICK

watch out! Beware of destroying one another.
GALATIANS 5:15 NLT

fyi booklist

read more about it...faith

- *Fuel: 10-Minute Devotions to Ignite the Faith of Parents and Teens*
  by Joe White

- *Checklist for Life for Teens*

- *12 Months of Faith*
  by Bettie Youngs

- *The Faith Difference: Prayers, Lessons, Activities and Games for Teens*
  by Kieran Sawyer

- *Teens Talkin' Faith: A Christian Perspective*
  by Michelle Trujillo

LET GOD TAKE YOU TO THE OTHER SIDE

The engineers hired to build a suspension bridge across the Niagara River faced a serious problem: how to get the first cable from one side of the river to the next. The river was too wide to throw a cable across it and too swift to cross by boat.

An engineer finally came up with a solution! With a favoring stiff wind, a kite was lofted and allowed to drift over the river and land on the opposite shore. Attached to the kite was a very light string, which was threaded through the kite's tip so that both ends of the string were in the hands of the kite flyer. Once the kite was in the hand of engineers on the far side, they re-moved the kite from its string and set up a pulley. A small rope was attached to one end of the original kite string and pulled across the river. At the end of this string, a piece of rope was attached and pulled across and so on until a cable strong enough to sustain the iron cable, which supported the bridge, could be drawn across the water.

Let your faith soar like that kite! Release it to God, believing that He can and will help you. When you link your released faith with patience and persistence, you will have what it takes to tackle virtually any problem.

> **Kites rise highest against the wind, not with it.**
> Winston Churchill

When the way is **rough**, your **patience** has a chance to **grow**. So let it **grow**, and **don't** try to **squirm** out of your problems.

JAMES 1:3-4 TLB

ALWAYS DO YOUR BEST

EVERY JOB IS A SELF-PORTRAIT OF THE PERSON WHO DOES IT. AUTOGRAPH YOUR WORK WITH EXCELLENCE.

LONG AGO, a band of minstrels lived in a faraway land. They traveled from town to town, singing and playing their music in hopes of making a living, but they had not been doing well financially. Times were hard, and the common people had little money to spend on concerts, even though their fee was small.

The group met one evening to discuss their plight. "I see no reason for opening tonight," one said. "It's snowing, and no one will come out on a night like this." Another said, "I agree. Last night we performed for just a handful. Even fewer will come tonight."

The leader of the troupe responded, "I know you are discouraged. I am too, but we have a responsibility to those who might come. We will go on, and we will do the best job of which we are capable. It is not the fault of those who come that others do not. They should not be punished with less than our best."

Heartened by his words, the minstrels gave their best performance ever. After the show, the old man called his troupe to him again. In his hand was a note, handed to him by one of the audience members just before the doors closed behind him. Slowly the man read, "Thank you for a beautiful performance." It was signed simply, "Your King."

Everything you do is performed before your king—the King of Kings. Are all of your words and deeds worthy of His audience?

Daniel **distinguished himself above** the governors and satraps, because an **excellent** **spirit** was in him.

DANIEL 6:3 NKJV

TOP **10** TIPS for Achieving Excellence

1. GIVE 100 PERCENT EFFORT TO ALL YOU DO.

2. DON'T SETTLE FOR LESS THAN YOUR BEST EFFORT.

3. CONSIDER MISTAKES FERTILE LEARNING SOIL.

4. LEARN FROM THE MISTAKES OF OTHERS AS WELL AS YOUR OWN.

5. NEVER GIVE UP.

6. ALWAYS BE TEACHABLE.

7. ASK FOR AND TAKE ADVICE FROM PEOPLE IN THE KNOW.

8. KEEP YOUR MORAL COMPASS POINTED TOWARD GOD.

9. DON'T WASTE YOUR TIME WITH ANGER AND IMPATIENCE.

10. PRACTICE THE FINE ART OF HUMILITY.

LOOK FOR EXAMPLES

FAMOUS WORLD WAR II general, George S. Patton Jr., was an avid reader and student of history. He wrote to his son in 1944: "To be a successful soldier, you must know history. Read it objectively. . . . In Sicily I decided as a result of my information, observations, and a sixth sense that I have that the enemy did not have another large scale attack in his system. I bet my shirt on that, and I was right." His sixth sense may very well have been formed by thousands of hours of reading history and both biographies and autobiographies.

Historical parallels were constantly on Patton's mind. When he observed the situation in Normandy on July 2, 1944, he immediately wrote Eisenhower that the German Schlieffen Plan of 1914 could be applied. A month later, an operation such as he had described brought about the German defeat in Normandy.

The book that perhaps influenced Patton most was Ardant du Picque's *Battle Studies*. Patton used it to help solve the problem of getting infantry to advance through enemy artillery fire. He recommended it to Eisenhower: "First read *Battle Studies* by Du Pique (you can get a copy at Leavenworth) then put your mind to a solution."

Most of the successful men in the world are avid readers, especially of biographies. If you are interested in being a success in life, immerse yourself in the life stories of successful people. You will learn from their mistakes and failures as well as their successes and triumphs.

> **Learn by experience— preferably other people's.**

All these things happened to them as examples—as object lessons to us—to warn us against doing the same things.

1 CORINTHIANS 10:11 TLB

new insights into ageless questions

It seems as if I'm always making stupid mistakes—crazy stuff that I should know better about, but somehow I don't. How can I learn from other people's mistakes without having to listen to a long, boring lecture?

Remember for a moment that your parents and grandparents were once your age, and while their generations looked and dressed differently, they dealt with the same basic issues you deal with. They are a remarkable resource of wisdom and counsel for you, and God has placed them right in front of you to give you the best possible chance of making good choices and avoiding painful mistakes.

Before you dismiss them as being out of touch with your reality, take the time to sit and talk with them about the difficult issues of life—things like morality, war, alcohol, drugs, sex, attitude, getting along with people, friendship, courage, relationships, money, the list is really endless. Really listen to what they have to say, keeping in mind that every mistake they made is one you can avoid if you are able to take hold of the lesson learned. You can also learn by observing what they did right and how it worked for them.

Sure, you can be stubborn and insist on learning everything the hard way, but that isn't God's best for you. Be smart by learning through the mistakes and successes of others.

CONSIDER THIS!

President John F. Kennedy loved to tell the tale of small boys in Ireland who would have footraces across the lush hills. When they came to a fence they were afraid to cross, they would challenge each other to throw their hats over first so they would feel compelled to go after them. Aiming for perfection is about throwing your hat over the fence into the future, so that you are inspired to follow it.

SHOOT FOR THE MOON

A young man who was confused about his future and in a quandary as to which direction to take with his life sat in a park, watching squirrels scamper among the trees. Suddenly a squirrel jumped from one high tree to another. It appeared to be aiming for a limb so far out of reach that the leap looked like suicide. As the young man had anticipated, the squirrel missed its mark; but it landed, safe and unconcerned, on a branch several feet lower. Then it climbed to its goal, and all was well.

An old man sitting on the other end of the bench remarked, "Funny, I've seen hundreds of 'em jump like that, especially when there are dogs all around

> **SHOOT FOR THE MOON. EVEN IF YOU MISS IT YOU WILL LAND AMONG THE STARS.**
>
> **LES BROWN**

and they can't come down to the ground. A lot of 'em miss, but I've never seen any hurt in trying." Then he chuckled and added, "I guess they've got to risk it if they don't want to spend their whole life in one tree."

The young man thought, *A squirrel takes a chance. Do I have less nerve than a squirrel?* He made up his mind in that moment to take the risk he had been thinking about. Sure enough, he landed safely, in a position higher than he had even dared to imagine.

What dream are you aiming for? Does it seem out of reach? Take a leap of faith. God will always catch you if you fall.

Aim for perfection.

2 CORINTHIANS 13:11 NIV

THINK ON THESE THINGS

In *A Closer Walk*, Catherine Marshall writes: "One morning last week He gave me an assignment: for one day I was to go on a 'fast' from criticism. I was not to criticize anybody about anything."

"For the first half of the day, I simply felt a void, almost as if I had been wiped out as a person. This was especially true at lunch. . . . I listened to the others and kept silent. . . . In our talkative family no one seemed to notice. Bemused, I noticed that my comments were not missed. The federal government, the judicial sytem, and the institutional church could apparently get along fine without my penetrating observations. But still I didn't see what this fast on criticism was accomplishing—until mid-afternoon."

> WHATEVER YOU DISLIKE IN ANOTHER PERSON, TAKE CARE TO CORRECT IN YOURSELF.
>
> THOMAS SPRAT

"That afternoon, a specific, positive vision for this life was dropped into my mind with God's unmistakable hallmark on it—joy! Ideas began to flow in a way I had not experienced in years. Now it was apparent what the Lord wanted me to see. My critical nature had not corrected a single one of the multitudinous things I found fault with. What it had done was to stifle my own creativity."

Before you are tempted to criticize someone, examine your own life. While you may not commit the same act or have the same habit you're about to criticize, you probably have some behavior that could be criticized. Don't stifle your creativity with criticism!

JESUS SAID, "WHY DO YOU LOOK AT THE SPECK OF SAWDUST IN YOUR BROTHER'S EYE AND PAY NO ATTENTION TO THE PLANK IN YOUR OWN EYE?"

MATTHEW 7:3 NIV

WISE WORDS

The truth is that for everything that can be accomplished by showing a person where he's wrong, ten times as much can be accomplished by showing him where he's right. The reason we don't do it so often is that it's more fun to throw a rock through a window than to put in a pane of glass.

ROBERT T. ALLEN

Facts

Archimedes was well aware of the remarkable possibilities furnished by his inventions of the lever and pulley. "Give me a place on which to stand," he famously declared, "and I will move the earth."

Hiero soon challenged the scientist to put his words to the test by helping sailors beach a large ship in the Syracusan fleet. Archimedes dutifully arranged a series of pulleys and cogs to such effect that he was able—single-handedly—to drag the enormous vessel from the water and onto the beach.

WHO SAYS IT'S IMPOSSIBLE?

Most of the **things** worth doing in the **world** had been **declared impossible** before they were done.

Louis D. Brandeis

Consider these examples of resistance to ideas and inventions that we now consider commonplace:

In Germany, experts proved that if trains went as fast as fifteen miles an hour—considered a frightful speed—blood would spurt from the travelers' noses and passengers would suffocate when going through tunnels. In the United States, experts said the introduction of the railroad would require the building of many insane asylums since people would be driven mad with terror at the sight of the locomotives.

The New York YWCA announced typing lessons for women in 1881, and vigorous protest erupted, on the grounds that the female constitution would break down under the strain.

When the idea of iron ships was proposed, experts insisted that they would not float, would damage more easily than wooden ships when grounding, that it would be difficult to preserve the iron bottom from rust, and that iron would play havoc with compass readings.

New Jersey farmers resisted the first successful cast-iron plow invented in 1797, claiming that the cast iron would poison the land and stimulate the growth of weeds.

Don't let the word "impossible" stop you. If inventors and visionaries had left every impossible task undone, our lives would be considerably more difficult. Nothing worth doing is impossible with the help of God!

With God all things are possible.

MATTHEW 19:26 NIV

LET GOOD REPLACE EVIL

Velazquez Polk and Janet Kuzmaak both grew up in Portland, Oregon, but the two could not have been more different. Polk was a tough street kid who joined a gang at age ten and was eventually arrested for selling drugs.

Kuzmaak was an honor roll student from an upper-class neighborhood. In 1980, Kuzmaak's sister was raped and strangled to death. Authorities never found her killer. She came to regard every criminal as her sister's murderer.

> **Flee from** youthful lusts and pursue righteousness . . . with those who call on the Lord from a pure heart.
>
> 2 TIMOTHY 2:22 NASB

Kuzmaak eventually became a nurse at a major medical center. Polk, released from jail in 1990, was given a job as her surgical aide. Kuzmaak was furious. She didn't believe in rehabilitation for criminals, but she noticed that when Polk's gang-member friends tried to entice him to rejoin their ranks, he refused. He told Kuzmaak he wanted to flee his old life and join a program to become a nurse's aide. She remembered that her sister had once befriended a man on parole, so she lobbied the hospital to pay Polk's tuition while she continued to monitor him.

Today, she and Polk are great friends. She helped him gain entrance into a world that he once did not know existed. He helped sweep away the bitterness that had once poisoned her heart.

Change and growth are always possible if you first turn away from evil, determined not to return.

When you flee temptations, don't leave a forwarding address.

☑ JUST DO IT

#1 In Matthew 5:44, Christ asks us to love our enemies, bless those who curse us, do good to those who hate us, and pray for those who use and persecute us. This month, identify five **#2** individuals who have wronged you, used you, or mistreated you and send them a postcard that:

1. forgives them.
#3 2. blesses them.
3. tells them God loves them.
4. offers your services to them.
#4 5. tells them you are praying for them.

Tough stuff, huh? That's the high calling of Christ.

#5

#8

HOW Do YOU MEASURE Up?

How do you "get back" at those who wrong you?

A. I feel hurt and avoid the person as long as possible.
B. I feel resentful and make sarcastic remarks when the opportunity arises.
C. I refuse to speak to the person until my anger diminishes.
D. I pray for the person who has wronged me and pray for God's grace and mercy on us both.
E. I'm never sure what to do.

Jesus gave His disciples specific instructions concerning how to treat those who had wronged them. Consider this passage from Matthew 5:38-42 (MSG).

"Here's another old saying that deserves a second look: 'Eye for eye, tooth for tooth.' Is that going to get us anywhere? Here's what I propose: 'Don't hit back at all. If someone strikes you, stand there and take it. If someone drags you into court and sues for the shirt off your back, giftwrap your best coat and make a present of it. And if someone takes unfair advantage of you, use the occasion to practice the servant life. No more tit-for-tat stuff. Live generously."

GET 'EM BACK WITH LOVE

WE TOO OFTEN LOVE THINGS AND USE PEOPLE, WHEN WE SHOULD BE USING THINGS AND LOVING PEOPLE.

One day, a boy at summer camp received a box of cookies from his mother. He ate a few, then placed the box under his bed. The next day, he discovered the cookies were gone. Later, a counselor who had been told of the theft saw a boy sitting behind a tree, eating the stolen cookies. He sought out the victim and said, "Bill, I know who stole your cookies. Will you help me teach him a lesson?" The boy replied, "Well, I guess—but aren't you going to punish him?"

The counselor said, "Not directly—that would only make him hate you. I have an idea; but first I want you to ask your mother to send some more cookies." The boy did as the counselor asked, and a few days later, another box of cookies arrived.

The counselor then said, "The boy who stole your cookies is by the lake. I suggest you go down there and share your cookies with him." The boy protested, "But he's the one who stole the first ones from me!" "I know," said the counselor. "Let's see what happens."

An hour later, the counselor saw the boys coming up the hill—the thief earnestly trying to get his new friend to accept his compass in payment for the stolen cookies, and the victim just as adamantly refusing, saying that a few old cookies didn't matter all that much!

Often, the best way to get back at someone is to show God's love. You can usually make a friend in the process.

Be devoted to one another in brotherly love.

Honor one another above yourselves.

ROMANS 12:10 NIV

Whoever heeds correction gains understanding.

PROVERBS 15:32 NIV

KEEP AN OPEN MIND

A FEUD DEVELOPED between two families who lived side by side in the mountains of Kentucky. It started when Grandpa Smith's cow jumped a stone fence and ate Grandpa Brown's corn. Brown shot the cow. A Smith boy then shot two Brown boys. The Browns shot one Smith. Bill Brown planned to kill a second Smith, but before he could, he was called away to war. While he was away, Bill's mother had a hard time making ends meet for her family, since Bill's father had been one of the victims.

At Christmas, the head of the Smith clan took his family to church. Usually he stayed outside, but this year it was so cold he went in to wait. The sermon was on Christ, the Prince of Peace, who died in our place for our sins. It struck him hard. He realized what a crime he had committed, repented, and then secretly hired a young boy to carry a basket of food to the Brown's home every day until Bill returned.

Once home, Bill set out to discover who had so generously helped his family. He followed the boy to the Smith's house, where Smith met him and said, "Shoot me, Bill, if you want to. But Christ has already died for my sins, and I hope you'll forgive me too." Bill did, and neighbors truly became neighbors again.

Never reach the point in life where you think you can't learn something new or change your opinion about something. You are never too old, or too young, to be forgiven.

Who's Who:

Peter

Peter was one of the first chosen by Jesus to be His disciple. A crusty fisherman, strong-willed, and impulsive, he seems like an odd choice. But Jesus saw something in the man. Peter made many mistakes during the three years he spent with Jesus. He was your typical act first, think-later type of guy.

But there was one last mistake for which Peter had no expectation of forgiveness. On the night Jesus was crucified, Peter betrayed His Lord. When asked if he was indeed one of Jesus' disciples, Peter denied ever having known Him.

Fortunately, Peter was man enough to learn from his mistake. He resisted the urge to run away, humbled himself, and stayed close within the body of believers. After His resurrection, Jesus forgave Peter and restored him . From that day forward, Peter served God resolutely, without faltering.

Don't let your mistakes put you out in the cold. Learn from them and then submit them to God, who will graciously forgive and restore you.

DON'T DELAY

THE WISE DOES AT ONCE WHAT THE FOOL DOES AT LAST.

AN OLD LEGEND recounts how Satan once called three of his top aides to a special meeting so that they might make a plan about how to stop the effectiveness of a particular group of Christians. One of the aides, Resentment, proposed, "We should convince them there is no God." Satan sneered at Resentment and replied, "That would never work. They know there's a God."

Bitterness then spoke up: "We'll convince them that God does not really care about right or wrong." Satan thought about the idea for a few moments but then rejected it. "Too many know that God does care," he finally said.

Malice then proposed his idea. "We'll let them go on thinking there is a God and that He cares about right and wrong, but we will keep whispering, 'There is no hurry, there is no hurry, there is no hurry.'"

Satan howled with delight! The plan was adopted, and Malice was promoted to an even higher position in Satan's malevolent hierarchy.

Who can tell how many souls have been lost or lives sorely wounded because someone has held to the commonly acceptable notion: Delay is okay.

Make hay while the sun shines—
that's smart; go fishing during
harvest—that's stupid.

PROVERBS 10:5 MSG

TOP 10 TIPS

for Avoiding Procrastination

1. GIVE YOURSELF A CLEAR DEADLINE.

2. CREATE ACTION STEPS AND COMPLETE ONE EACH DAY.

3. COMPLETE DIFFICULT AND DREADED TASKS BEFORE EASY ONES.

4. ENVISION THE TASK COMPLETED.

5. DON'T OVERLOAD.

6. ASK GOD FOR A WINNING ATTITUDE.

7. ASK SOMEONE TO HELP YOU BE ACCOUNTABLE.

8. TAKE ADVANTAGE OF THE POWER OF HABIT, BY DOING SOMETHING THE SAME WAY AT THE SAME TIME FOR TWENTY-ONE DAYS IN A ROW.

9. WHEN YOU OVERCOME PROCRASTINATION IN AN AREA, GIVE YOURSELF A CLEAR AND APPEALING REWARD.

10. COMMIT YOURSELF TO THE LORD ANEW EACH MORNING.

GIVE WITH BOTH HANDS

For years, Arthur Blessit has carried a six-by-ten-foot, eighty-pound cross on his shoulders through towns and cities around the world. "It blows people's minds," he says. Once he has gained their attention, he finds he has a unique opportunity to share the Gospel.

Blessit first became well known for preaching to the hippies of Hollywood's Sunset Strip. He gained national attention when he undertook a cross-carrying journey—along with four members of his rock group, the Eternal Rush—to Washington, D.C. The 3,500-mile trip took seven months to complete.

As the group traveled, they held rallies. Blessit urged fellow Christians to meet him at the Washington Monument at the end of his trip—but not with empty hands. "Christians need to come and give something," he preached. He asked that people bring or send two gifts for the nation's needy, gifts given openly with both hands. Those who went to the capital to meet him found a third opportunity to give. This gift was to be made with an open heart and an open vein—at a bloodmobile parked on the site.

While the gospel message is free to all who will receive it, the giving of the Gospel costs, and continues to cost, a great deal!

THE BEST THINGS IN LIFE ARE NOT FREE.

YOU WERE NOT REDEEMED WITH PERISHABLE THINGS LIKE SILVER OR GOLD . . . BUT WITH PRECIOUS BLOOD, AS OF A LAMB UNBLEMISHED AND SPOTLESS, THE BLOOD OF CHRIST.

1 PETER 1:18-19 NASB

WISE WORDS

During a visit to Korea, two American
businessmen were highly amused to see a
young farmer pulling a plow, guided by his
father. On recounting the story to a missionary,
they learned this father and son were Christians
who sold their only ox and contributed the
money to their church for a new building.
One of the men responded in an awed voice,
"What a stupendous sacrifice!"
The missionary replied, "They did not feel
that way about it. They counted it a great joy
that they had an ox to give to the Lord's work."

WALTER SCHLICHTING

CONSIDER THIS!

What is the price of salvation? Forgiveness of sin and the invitation to live a life of peace and joy with God for eternity is a great gift. Like the word "gift" implies, it is free. But that does not mean that salvation is free or even cheap to the giver. John 3:16 sums up the incredible cost for our redemption. It says: "God so loved the world that He gave His only begotten Son, that whoever believes in Him should not perish but have everlasting life."

God gave His Son for you, sending Him to earth to live as a mere human and carry the message of God's love and forgiveness to a lost and dying world.

His Son, Jesus, was ridiculed, beaten, tortured, and crucified—that was the unspeakably precious cost of your salvation. You can't honor His gift with a cheap commitment. You owe Him the best that you can give.

CHRIST-LIKE LIVING

In an extensive opinion survey, "The Day America Told the Truth," James Patterson and Peter Kim reported some startling findings:

- Only 13 percent saw all Ten Commandments as binding and relevant.
- 91 percent lied regularly, both at work and home.
- Most workers admitted to goofing off an average of seven hours a week.
- About half of the workforce admitted they regularly called in sick even when they felt well.

When they were asked what they would be willing to do for $10 million, 25 percent said they would abandon their families, 23 percent would be prostitutes for a week, and 7 percent would murder a stranger!

Lest you conclude that the people they surveyed were all ungodly criminals, two other statisticians, William Hendricks and Doug Sherman, found that Christians were almost as likely as unbelievers to do such things as steal from the workplace, falsify their income tax, and selectively obey laws.

To truly claim to be a Christian, a person must do far more than go to church occasionally. He or she must strive to be Christ-like 24 hours a day, 365 days a year, in all situations and all circumstances.

> **IF A MAN CANNOT BE A CHRISTIAN IN THE PLACE WHERE HE IS, HE CANNOT BE A CHRISTIAN ANYWHERE.**
>
> HENRY WARD BEECHER

Don't work hard only when your master is watching and then shirk when he isn't looking; work hard and with gladness all the time, as though working for Christ, doing the will of God with all your hearts.

EPHESIANS 6:6-7 TLB

booklist

- **Debt-Free Living: How to Get Out of Debt (And Stay Out)**
  by Larry Burkett

- **Master Your Money**
  by Ron Blue

- **Money Matters for Teens Workbook: Age 15-18**
  by Larry Burkett, Todd Temple

- **Personal Finance for Dummies**
  by Eric Tyson

- **Rich Dad Poor Dad for Teens: The Secrets About Money—That You Don't Learn in School!**
  by Robert T. Kiyosaki, Sharon L. Lechter

DEBT IS A HARD TASKMASTER

At the age of twenty-four, financial advisor and author Ron Blue felt he had everything he needed to be successful—an MBA degree, a CPA certificate, and a prestigious position in the New York City office of the world's largest CPA firm. Then at the age of thirty-two, he committed his life to Jesus Christ and began to see life from a new perspective. When he decided to establish his own financial advisory firm, he used his skills to develop a business plan and arrange for a ten-thousand-dollar line of credit at a bank. Almost immediately, however, he felt convicted that God did not want him to borrow money to start his business. He canceled the credit line, not knowing what to do next but knowing he was not to go into debt.

One day, while explaining his business idea to a friend, the friend said, "Would you consider designing a financial seminar for our executives who are getting ready to retire?" Ron jumped at the opportunity. His friend was the training director for a large company, and the company agreed to pay six thousand dollars in advance for development of the seminar, then one thousand dollars each for four seminars during the year. Ron had the ten thousand dollars he needed without borrowing a dime.

Do your best to stay out of debt. You'll feel much freer, and God will bless you for trusting in Him.

> **Money is a good servant but a bad master.**
> Frances Bacon

The **rich** rules over the **poor**, and the **borrower** is servant to the lender.

PROVERBS 22:7 NKJV

DIG FOR THE FACTS

TED TURNER IS ONE OF the conspicuous personalities of the twentieth century. He turned Channel 17 in Atlanta into the first "Super Station," transmitting its signal to cable systems nationwide via satellite. Soon after, he purchased the Atlanta Braves baseball team and the Atlanta Hawks basketball team. In 1980, he originated CNN, the world's first live, 'round-the-clock, all-news television network. He organized the Inaugural Goodwill Olympic Games in Moscow, has won numerous awards, and has held national and world sailing titles.

About making choices and decisions, Ted has given this advice, "There is a saying, 'Be sure of your information, then go ahead.' My father was the first one who pointed this out to me. . . . Get all the information you can, along with the advice and counsel of people you think are wise. This is a prerequisite for success in the long haul. You should not make decisions until you have complete knowledge about things. [When] you have to form opinions without as much information as you should have, or without firsthand knowledge . . . don't hold hard and fast opinions. When new information becomes available, you should be able to change your mind."

That is wise advice. Jumped-to conclusions are usually based on speculation—not truth. The person who comes out on top is going to be the one who not only knows all the facts but most importantly, knows the truth.

lighten up

An editor once admonished his cub reporter, Mark Twain, never to state as fact anything to which he could not personally attest. Twain complied, composing this classic account of a certain (not so certain) gala social event:

"A woman giving the name of Mrs. James Jones, who is reported to be one of the society leaders of the city, is said to have given what purported to be a party yesterday to a number of alleged ladies. The hostess claims to be the wife of a reputed attorney."

Be diligent to present yourself approved to God, a rightly dividing the word of truth.

"Jumping to conclusions is not half as good an exercise as digging for facts."

worker who does not need to be ashamed,
2 TIMOTHY 2:15 NKJV

Facts

What caused Peter to sink when he walked on the water toward Jesus?

He took his eyes off Jesus and looked down at the water. Read the following story from *The Message:*

As soon as the meal was finished, he insisted that the disciples get in the boat and go on ahead to the other side while he dismissed the people. With the crowd dispersed, he climbed the mountain so he could be by himself and pray. He stayed there alone, late into the night.

Meanwhile, the boat was far out to sea when the wind came up against them and they were battered by the waves. At about four o'clock in the morning, Jesus came toward them walking on the water. They were scared out of their wits. "A ghost!" they said, crying out in terror. But Jesus was quick to comfort them. "Courage, it's me. Don't be afraid."

Peter, suddenly bold, said, "Master, if it's really you, call me to come to you on the water."

He said, "Come ahead."

Jumping out of the boat, Peter walked on the water to Jesus. But when he looked down at the waves churning beneath his feet, he lost his nerve and started to sink. He cried, "Master, save me!"

Jesus didn't hesitate. He reached down and grabbed his hand. Then he said, "Faint-heart, what got into you?"

KEEP YOUR EYES ON JESUS

Obstacles are those **frightful things** you see
when you take your **eyes off** the goal.

Henry Ford

During the darkest days of the Civil War, the hopes of the Union nearly died. When certain goals seemed unreachable, the leaders of the Union turned to President Abraham Lincoln for solace, guidance, and encouragement. Once when a delegation called at the White House and detailed a long list of crises facing the nation, Lincoln told this story:

"Years ago a young friend and I were out one night when a shower of meteors fell from the clear November sky. The young man was frightened, but I told him to look up in the sky past the shooting stars to the fixed stars beyond, shining serene in the firmament, and I said, 'Let us not mind the meteors, but let us keep our eyes on the stars.'"

When times are troubled or life seems to be changing too fast, keep your inner eyes of faith and hope on those things that you know to be lasting and sure. Don't limit your gaze to what you know, but focus on whom you know. God alone—and a relationship with Him that is eternal—is the supreme goal. He never changes, and He cannot be removed from His place as the King of Glory.

Peter . . . walked on the water toward Jesus.

When [Peter] looked
around at the high waves,
he was terrified and began
to sink.

MATTHEW 14:30 TLB

HAVE THINE OWN WAY, LORD

During a prayer meeting one night, an elderly woman pleaded, "It really doesn't matter what You do with us, Lord, just have Your way with our lives." Adelaide Pollard, a rather well-known itinerant Bible teacher, overheard her prayer. At the time, she was deeply discouraged because she had been unable to raise the money she needed to go to Africa for missionary service. She was moved by this woman's sincere request of God, and when she went home that evening, she meditated on Jeremiah 18:3-4:

"Then I went down to the potter's house, and, behold, he wrought a work on the wheels. And the vessel that he made of clay was marred in the hand of the potter: so he made it again another vessel, as seemed good to the potter to make it."

Before retiring, Adelaide took pen in hand and wrote in hymn form her own prayer:

"Have Thine own way, Lord! Have Thine own way! Thou art the potter, I am the clay. Mold me and make me after Thy will, while I am waiting, yielded and still.

"Have Thine own way, Lord! Have Thine own way! Search me, and try me, Master, today! Whiter than snow, Lord, wash me just now, as in Thy presence humbly I bow."

The best way to discover the purpose for your life and how to do it is to give your whole life to God. Then He can fulfill His plan for you.

After this manner therefore pray ye. . . .

DON'T ASK GOD FOR WHAT YOU THINK IS GOOD; ASK HIM FOR WHAT HE THINKS IS GOOD FOR YOU.

YOUR KINGDOM COME. YOUR WILL BE DONE, ON EARTH AS IT IS IN HEAVEN.

MATTHEW 6:10 NASB

WISE WORDS

When we leave God out of our reckoning, difficulties will daunt us, temptation will triumph over us, sin will seduce us, self will sway us, the world will warp us, seeming impossibilities will irritate us, unbelief will undermine our faith, Christian work will worry us, fear will frighten us, and all things will wear a somber hue. But when God is recognized as the One who undertakes for us, then difficulties are opportunities to trust Him, temptations are the harbingers of victory, sin has no attraction, self is denied, unbelief is ignored, service is a delight, contentment sings in the heart, and all things are possible.

F.E. MARSH

HOW Do YOU MEASURE Up?

Do you try to impress others by creating an image that is not altogether true? For instance, do you:

A. Try to live up to the affluence of your friends' families?
B. Make unfair demands on your family's finances to live up to this affluent image you've created?
C. Tell others "little white lies" to make yourself seem successful?
D. Become a name dropper?
E. Remain comfortable with who you are and content with your position in life?

If you said "yes" to any of the first four choices, you may need to take a serious look at why you feel compelled to impress others. God created you to be a unique individual with a beauty, purpose, and personality all your own. He wants you to be comfortable in your own skin, rather than desperate to be someone else. Ask Him to help you applaud the person you were meant to be.

WHOM ARE YOU TRYING TO IMPRESS?

DEFINITION OF STATUS: BUYING SOMETHING YOU DON'T NEED WITH MONEY YOU DON'T HAVE TO IMPRESS PEOPLE YOU DON'T LIKE.

DR. EUGENE SWEARINGEN

Guy de Maupassant's *The Necklace* is the story of a young woman, Mathilde, who desires desperately to be accepted into high society. One day her husband, an ordinary man, is given an invitation to an elegant ball. Mathilde borrows a necklace from a wealthy friend to wear to the occasion. During the course of the evening, she receives many compliments from the aristocracy present. Unfortunately, later that night, she realizes she has lost the necklace.

In order to restore the lost jewelry, Mathilde's husband borrows 36,000 francs, tapping every resource available to him. A look-alike necklace is created, and Mathilde gives it to her friend, without telling her what had happened.

For ten years, the couple slaves to pay back the borrowed francs, each of them working two jobs. They are forced to sell their home and live in a slum. One day after the debt has finally been paid, Mathilde runs into her well-to-do friend. She confesses that the necklace she returned is not the one she borrowed, and she learns that the necklace loaned to her had been made from fake gemstones! The borrowed necklace had been worth less than 500 francs.

Trying to keep up appearances almost always leads to falling flat on your face.

Jesus said, "They do all their **deeds** to be noticed by **men**."

MATTHEW 23:5 NASB

THE LESSON FROM THE BEE

MANY PEOPLE TODAY SEEM to go through their day with their stingers out, ready to attack others or to defend their position at the slightest provocation. We all do well, however, to consider the full nature of the bees we sometimes seem to emulate.

Bees readily feed each other, sometimes even a bee of a different colony. The worker bees feed the queen bee, who cannot feed herself. They feed the drones during their period of usefulness in the hive. They feed the young. They seem to enjoy this social act of mutual feeding.

Bees cluster together for warmth in cold weather and fan their wings to cool the hive in hot weather, thus working for one another's comfort.

When the time comes for bees to move to new quarters, scouts report back to the group, doing a dance very similar to the one used to report a find of honey. When enough scouts have confirmed the suitability of the new location, the bees appear to make a common decision, take wing, and migrate together—all at the same time—in what we call a swarm.

Only as a last-resort measure of self-defense do bees engage their stingers and then, never against their fellow bees. We would do well to learn from them!

> **The most important single ingredient in the formula of success is knowing how to get along with people.**
> THEODORE ROOSEVELT

See that no one pays back evil for evil, but always try to do good to each other and to everyone else.

1 THESSALONIANS 5:15 TLB

new insights into ageless questions

I thought Christians were supposed to be like Jesus, acting like He would act if He were here on earth. But all I see is Christians fighting and arguing with each other. My friends say that Christians are just a bunch of hypocrites when they talk about peace and love. What am I supposed to say to them?

When people accept Jesus as their Savior and become Christians, they are forgiven—not perfect. In fact, the Bible says they are just like newborn babies. Now you know that babies have a lot more potential than they do good sense. Typically, they scream for what they want and are selfish (though adorable) little creatures. Newborn Christians often act badly as well. That's why the apostle Paul keeps telling the Christians in the New Testament to grow up and start acting more like Jesus.

Unfortunately, some Christians never do shed their baby ways. That's certainly not God's will, but He loves them just the same. And He never stops forgiving them and trying to teach them a better way to live.

The best thing you can do is to keep growing in your faith and living a life that is pleasing to your Heavenly Father. When your friends see that, they will learn that all Christians don't behave badly. The vast majority really are committed to peace and love.

CONSIDER THIS!

How Do You Spell Patience?

Persistence pays off!

Always keep your goals in sight.

Train yourself to approach your goals one step at a time.

Invest your whole self into your efforts.

Experience the joys of hard work.

Never give up!

Celebrate smalls steps toward success.

Expect the best from your successes and your failures.

LET YOUR PATIENCE WORK FOR YOU

We often think of great artists and musicians as having bursts of genius. More often, they are models of painstaking patience. Their greatest works tend to have been accomplished over long periods and in extreme hardships.

Beethoven is said to have rewritten each bar of his music at least a dozen times.

Josef Haydn produced more than eight hundred musical compositions before writing *The Creation,* the oratorio for which he is most famous.

Michelangelo's "Last Judgment" is considered one of the twelve master paintings of the ages. It took him eight years to complete. He produced more than two thousand sketches and renderings in the process.

PATIENCE IS BITTER BUT ITS FRUIT IS SWEET.

Leonardo da Vinci worked on "The Last Supper" for ten years, often working so diligently that he forgot to eat.

When he was quite elderly, the pianist Ignace Paderewski was asked by an admirer, "Is it true that you still practice every day?" He replied, "Yes, at least six hours a day." The admirer said in awe, "You must have a world of patience." Paderewski said, "I have no more patience than the next fellow. I just use mine."

Put your patience to use in the pursuit of your dreams.

You have **need** of **endurance,**

so that **after** you have **done** the **will of God,**

you may **receive** the **promise.**

HEBREWS 10:36 NKJV

GET BACK UP

> THE MAN WHO WINS MAY HAVE BEEN COUNTED OUT SEVERAL TIMES, BUT HE DIDN'T HEAR THE REFEREE.
>
> H.E. JANSEN

THE DIFFERENCE between success and failure is often the ability to get up just one more time than you fall down!

Moses easily could have given up. He had an interrupted childhood and lived with a foster family. He also had a strong temper, a stammering tongue, and a criminal record, but when God called to him, he ultimately said yes.

Joshua had seen the Promised Land and then been forced to wander in the wilderness for forty years with cowards who didn't believe, as he did, that they could conquer their enemies and possess the land. He could have given up in discouragement, but he was willing to go when God said to go.

Peter had a hard time making the transition from fisherman to fisher of men. He sank while trying to walk on water, was strongly rebuked by Jesus for trying to tell Him what to do, and denied knowing Jesus in that hour when Jesus needed him most. He easily could have seen himself as a hopeless failure, but when the opportunity came to preach the Gospel before thousands on the Day of Pentecost, he responded.

No matter what you've done, what mistakes you may have made, what errors you may have committed, you're not a failure until you lie down and quit.

Though a **righteous man** falls seven times, he **rises again**.

PROVERBS 24:16 NIV

TOP 10 TIPS for Challenging Your Perception of Failures

1. REMOVE THE "YOU" FROM FAILURE.

2. TAKE ACTION AND REDUCE YOUR FEAR.

3. CHANGE YOUR RESPONSE TO FAILURE BY ACCEPTING RESPONSIBILITY.

4. DON'T LET THE FAILURE FROM OUTSIDE GET INSIDE YOU.

5. SAY GOOD-BYE TO YESTERDAY.

6. CHANGE YOURSELF, AND YOUR WORLD CHANGES.

7. GET OVER YOURSELF AND START GIVING YOURSELF.

8. FIND THE BENEFIT IN EVERY BAD EXPERIENCE.

9. IF AT FIRST YOU DO SUCCEED, TRY SOMETHING HARDER.

10. LEARN FROM A BAD EXPERIENCE AND MAKE IT A GOOD EXPERIENCE.

A person without self-control is as defenseless as a city with BROKEN–DOWN walls.

PROVERBS 25:28 NLT

DEVELOP "WON'T" POWER

IN *SIN, SEX AND SELF-CONTROL,* Norman Vincent Peale writes: "Martha took the kids away to the mountains for a month, so I was a summer bachelor. And about midway through that month I met a girl, a beautiful girl looking for excitement. She made it clear that I had a green light . . . so for one weekend I put my conscience in mothballs and arranged a meeting with her for Saturday night.

"I woke up early Saturday morning with a bit of a hangover; I'd played poker until late the night before. I decided to get up, put on my swimming trunks, and take a walk on the beach to clear my head. I took an ax along, because the wreck of an old barge had come ashore down the beach, and there was a lot of tangled rope that was worth salvaging. . . . There was something about the freshness of the morning and the feel of the ax that made me want to keep on swinging it. So I began to chop in earnest."

As he chopped, a strange thing began to happen. He said, "I felt as if I were outside myself, looking at myself through a kind of fog that was gradually clearing. And suddenly I knew that what I had been planning for that evening was so wrong, so out of key with my standards and my loyalties and the innermost me that it was out of the question." He canceled the date.

Have you exercised your "won't" power lately?

Who's Who:

Robert E. Lee

The great Civil War General Robert E. Lee became the commander in chief of the Confederate Armies in the winter of 1865. Soon after, he returned to his hometown of Richmond, Virginia, a paroled prisoner of war, who chose to spend the rest of his life setting an example for thousands of other ex-Confederates.

Toward the end of his heroic, tragic life, the great man attended the christening of a friend's child. The mother asked him for a word that would guide the child along the road to manhood. Lee's answer summed up the creed that had borne him, through struggle and suffering, to a great place in American history. "Teach him," he said simply, "to deny himself."

PASS OUT SOME SMILES AND THOUGHTFUL WORDS

It has been estimated that more than 95 percent of all Americans receive at least one or more Christmas cards each year. The average is actually more than seventy cards per family! Millions of cards are mailed worldwide each holiday season. Have you ever wondered where this custom began?

A museum director in the mid-nineteenth century had a personal habit of sending notes to his friends at Christmastime each year, just to wish them a joyful holiday season. One year, he found he had little time to write, yet he still wanted to send a message of good cheer. He asked his friend, John Horsely, to design a card that he might sign and send. Those who received the cards loved them so much they created cards of their own. Thus the Christmas card was invented!

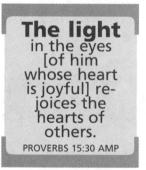

The light in the eyes [of him whose heart is joyful] rejoices the hearts of others.
PROVERBS 15:30 AMP

It's often the simple heartfelt gestures in life that speak most loudly of friendship. Ask yourself today, What can I do to bring a smile to the face of a friend? What can I do to bring good cheer into the life of someone who is in need, trouble, sickness, or sorrow? Follow through on your answer. It's not a gift you are giving as much as a friendship you are building!

Good nature begets smiles, smiles beget friends, and friends are better than a fortune.

DAVID DUNN

☑ JUST DO IT

#1 **Don't wait for the holidays to send greetings to your friends.**

#2 This week make a list with names of all those whose friend-ship you cherish. Each week take two or three of the names and send them a friendship card or letter telling them what you like most about them. Also let them know that you are praying for them especially that week for God to guide their paths into a closer relationship with Him.

#3 Once those words are written, don't forget to do what you've promised. Keep the list of names with you in your wallet or purse and pull them out whenever you can. Pray a simple prayer—it's fine for it to be silent—for each person on the list.

#4

#5

#6

#7

HANG IN THERE

We all know the power of gravity. When we drop a hammer, it hits our toes; it never floats upward. We fall down not up. What many of us don't realize is that the gravitational energy of the whole earth has been estimated to amount to only a millionth of a horsepower! A toy magnet in the hands of a child probably has thousands of times more energy.

What gravity lacks in energy, however, it makes up in tenacity. Gravity simply refuses to let go.

Not only is gravity tenacious, but it has far-reaching effects. Gravitational pull appears to be virtually limitless, reaching across the universe with nearly unimaginable power. Gravitational pull is what keeps the moon orbiting the earth, the planets revolving around the sun, and the sun—along with a billion other stars—rotating around the center of our galaxy like a cosmic pinwheel.

You may not have a great deal of power or energy today, but as the popular phrase states, you can "hang in there."

Don't stop believing! Don't give up hope! Eventually the door will be opened.

> PERSEVERANCE IS A GREAT ELEMENT OF SUCCESS; IF YOU ONLY KNOCK LONG ENOUGH AND LOUD ENOUGH AT THE GATE, YOU ARE SURE TO WAKE UP SOMEBODY.
> HENRY WADSWORTH LONGFELLOW

"ASK, AND IT WILL BE GIVEN TO YOU; SEEK, AND YOU WILL FIND; KNOCK, AND IT WILL BE OPENED TO YOU."
LUKE 11:9 NKJV

WISE WORDS

’Tis a lesson you should heed,
Try, try again.
If at first you don’t succeed,
Try, try again.
Then your courage should appear,
For, if you will persevere,
You will conquer, never fear;
Try, try again.

WILLIAM EDWARD HICKSON

booklist

read more about it...prayer

- *Life on the Edge: A Young Adult's Guide to a Meaningful Future*
  by Dr. James Dobson

- *Hot Topics–Tough Questions*
  by Bill Myers

- *E-mail from God for Teens*
  by Claire and Curt Cloninger

- *God's Little Instruction Book for Teens*
  by Honor Books

LET'S GO!

A MAN ONCE TOOK HIS three-year-old daughter to an amusement park. It was her first visit to such a place, and she was in awe at the sights and sounds, but mostly she was thrilled at the whirl and whiz of the rides. She begged her dad to let her ride one particular ride, even though it was considered the scariest ride for kids her age. As she whipped around the corners in her kiddy car, she suddenly wrinkled up her face and let loose with a terrified cry. Her father, who was riding in the car with her, struggled to get her attention. With a big smile, he shouted over the roar of the ride, "This is fun!" When the little girl saw that he was not terrified, she began to laugh. The new experience that was initially terrifying had suddenly become enjoyable. In fact, she insisted on riding the same ride three more times!

What a comfort it is to know that not only will our Heavenly Father will not only ride the new rides in life with us, but the future is never scary to Him. He has good things planned for us. When we look into the future from our perspective, we may become frightened. When we look at the future from God's perspective, we are far more likely to shout, "Let's go! Isn't this going to be fun?"

> I like the dreams of the future better than the history of the past.
>
> THOMAS JEFFERSON

Do not **remember** the former things, Nor **consider** the things of old. Behold, I will do a **new thing**.

ISAIAH 43:18-19 NKJV

Fun Facts

As a young man, Thomas Edison's primary interest was improving the telegraph. He invented the multiplex telegraph, the ticker tape machine, and other telegraphic innovations. In the early 1870s, financier Jay Gould bought out the Western Union telegraph system, establishing a monopoly of the industry. Edison realized that the lack of competition reduced his need to be innovative.

Edison described this realization as a "whack on the side of the head" that knocked him out of his telegraphic routine of thinking, forcing him to look into other areas to use his talents. Within just a few years, he came up with the light bulb, the power plant, the phonograph, the film projector, and several other inventions.

DO THE COMMON THINGS WELL

The secret of **success** is to do
the **common** things **uncommonly** well.

John D. Rockefeller Jr.

Helping the deaf to communicate was Alexander Graham Bell's motivation for his life's work, perhaps because his mother and wife were both deaf. "If I can make a deaf-mute talk," Bell said, "I can make metal talk." For five frustrating and impoverished years, he experimented with a variety of materials in an effort to make a metal disk that, vibrating in response to sound, could reproduce those sounds and send them over an electrified wire.

During a visit to Washington, D.C., he called on Joseph Henry, a scientist who was a pioneer in research related to electricity. He presented his ideas to him and asked his advice: Should he let someone else perfect the telephone, or should he do it himself? Henry encouraged him to do it himself, to which Bell complained that he lacked the necessary knowledge of electricity. Henry's brief solution was, "Get it."

So Bell studied electricity. A year later when he obtained a patent for the telephone, the officials in the patent office credited him with knowing more about electricity than all the other inventors of his day combined.

Hard work. Study. Hope. Persistence. These are all common things. They are the keys, however, to doing uncommonly well.

Do you see a man who excels in his
work? He will stand before kings; he
will not stand before unknown men.

PROVERBS 22:29 NKJV

PASS THE TEST

THE KOH-IN-NOOR diamond is among the world's most spectacular. It is part of the British crown jewels, presented to Queen Victoria by a maharajah in India when the maharajah was only a young boy.

Years later, when he was a grown man, the maharajah visited Queen Victoria in England. He asked that the stone be brought from the Tower of London, where it was kept in safety, to Buckingham Palace. The queen did as he requested.

Taking the diamond in his hand, he knelt before the queen and presented it back to her, saying, "Your Majesty, I gave this jewel when I was a child, too young to know what I was doing.

lighten up

At a dinner held in his honor one evening, Harvard president Charles W. Eliot was regaled by toasts from several professors.

"Since you became president," one colleague enthused, "Harvard has become a storehouse of knowledge."

"What you say is true, but I can claim little credit for it," Eliot replied. "It is simply that the freshmen bring so much in and the seniors take so little away."

I want to give it to you again in the fullness of my strength, with all of my heart and affection, and gratitude, now and forever, fully realizing all that I do."

A day will come when you likely will look back and say, "I'm grateful for my teachers and the lessons they taught me about discipline, concentration, hard work, cooperation, and the right and wrong ways to compete." Even more valuable will be the day when you look in a mirror and say, "Knowing what I now know about life, I see value in continuing to teach these lessons to myself."

> "School seeks to get you ready for examination; life gives the finals."

the faith; test yourselves. 2 CORINTHIANS 13:5 NIV

CONSIDER THIS!

How do you spell passion? Take some tim to ponder these points about passion.

Pursue your vision and dream.

Answer God's call on your life.

Seek God's will.

Seize opportunities.

Initiate contacts who can help you.

Open your heart to possibilities.

Never give up—think positive thoughts.

PASSIONATE ENTHUSIASM

After years of working in Rome on life-size sculptures, Michelangelo went to Florence, where a large block of splendid white Carrara marble had been obtained for a colossal statue. Within weeks, he had signed an agreement to complete a rendition of David for the cathedral. Contract in hand, he started in at once, working with a furious energy so great that he often slept in his clothes, resenting the time it took to take them off and put them on again. He faultlessly examined and precisely measured the marble to see what pose it could accommodate. He made sketches of possible attitudes and careful, detailed drawings from models. He tested his ideas in wax on a small scale. When he was finally satisfied with his design, only then did he pick up a chisel and mallet. Michelangelo approached painting the ceiling of the Sistine Chapel with the same intensity. He took only a month to develop the theme, then launched with a fury into the final design, building scaffolding, and hiring helpers. Lying at uncomfortable angles on hard boards, breathing the suffocating air just under the vault—plaster dust inflaming his eyes and irritating his skin—he spent much of the next four years literally sweating in physical distress as he worked. May you do your work with the same passionate enthusiasm!

> **NOTHING GREAT WAS EVER ACHIEVED WITHOUT ENTHUSIASM.**
>
> RALPH WALDO EMERSON

The joy of GOD is your strength!

NEHEMIAH 8:10 MSG

MANNERS MATTER

> ## POLITENESS GOES FAR, YET COSTS NOTHING.
>
> SENECA

IN 1865, AFTER General Ulysses S. Grant had moved his occupying army into Shiloh, he ordered a seven o'clock curfew for the city. One distinguished Southern lady, a Mrs. Johnson, was seen walking near the army's downtown headquarters near the curfew time.

General Grant approached her and said, "Mrs. Johnson, it's a little dangerous out there. I am going to ask two of my officers to escort you home."

She replied determinedly, "I won't go."

Grant smiled, went back into his headquarters, and returned in a few minutes, wearing an overcoat that covered his insignia and rank, and therefore the fact that he was a Northerner.

"May I walk with you, Mrs. Johnson?" he asked.

"Why, yes," Mrs. Johnson replied, nearly blushing. "I'm always glad to have a gentleman as an escort."

Mrs. Johnson would walk with a man she saw as a gentleman, even though she would not walk with a Union solider. Good manners and genuine politeness go a long way toward "covering" many of our faults, mistakes, and differences.

A kind man benefits himself.

PROVERBS 11:17 NIV

TOP 10 TIPS for Being All Things to All People

1. BEFRIEND AN UNPOPULAR STUDENT AT SCHOOL.

2. SEND AN ENCOURAGING POSTCARD TO SOMEONE WHO IS ILL.

3. DO A CHORE FOR A SENIOR CITIZEN.

4. OFFER SOMEONE A GENUINE COMPLIMENT.

5. VISIT SOMEONE WHO NEEDS A FRIEND.

6. OFFER TO BABYSIT FOR A SINGLE MOTHER.

7. REMIND SOMEONE THAT YOU LOVE THEM.

8. OFFER TO CLEAN THE KITCHEN AFTER DINNER.

9. DON'T FORGET TO BE KIND TO YOUR OWN FAMILY.

10. MAKE A LIST OF TEN KINDNESSES TO DO FOR OTHERS NEXT WEEK.

HOW Do YOU MEASURE Up?

Are you taking full advantage of your educational opportunities?

When my teacher gives me an assignment, do I:
A. Procrastinate, then slap something together at the last minute?
B. Begin my work early and pace myself to meet my deadline?
C. Blow off the assignment altogether? It won't prepare me for the future anyway.
D. Tackle the project with passion and give it 100 percent?

When grades come out, I am:
A. Nervous, wondering whether or not my grades are passing.
B. Prepared to hide my grades from my parents, hoping they won't notice.
C. Hopeful that my teachers will have mercy on me and give me a better grade than I've earned.
D. Proud to accept the grades I've been given, knowing that I did my best.

If you answered the questions with a "D," then you will probably go on to do great things academically. If you answered any of the others, you are risking your education and your future. Correct your course while there is still time.

LEARN TO BE A THINKER

> ## YOU CAN LEAD A BOY TO COLLEGE, BUT YOU CANNOT MAKE HIM THINK.
>
> KIN HUBBARD

At Princeton, Woodrow Wilson was first a teacher and later president of the university. Although he was popular with the students, he did have a reputation for cracking down on students who were not serious in their pursuit of an education.

The mother of one young man who was expelled for cheating made a trip to Princeton to talk with Wilson. She pleaded with him to reinstate her son because of the possible adverse reaction his expulsion would have on her own health and reputation. She told him of an impending operation and said she felt certain she would die if her son were not readmitted. Wilson heard her pleas and then responded, taking a very tough stance, "Madam, you force me to say a hard thing. If I had to choose between your life or my life or anybody's life and the good of this college, I should choose the good of the college."

Failure to study and to apply oneself fully to one's studies is a form of rebellion. The same holds for cheating. Do your best in school. Don't blame a teacher for being too hard on you, when the blame actually lies in your being too easy on yourself. Learn to be a thinker!

It is **senseless** to pay tuition to **educate** a **rebel** who has **no heart for truth.**

PROVERBS 17:16 TLB

MATURITY

A number of definitions of maturity have been offered by experts, but these are perhaps among the best understood by the average person:

• Maturity is when you not only want to have a puppy to call your own, but when you remember on your own to give it food and water every day.

• Maturity is when you not only know how to dress yourself, but you remember to put your dirty clothes in the laundry hamper after you've taken them off.

• Maturity is when you not only are capable of using a telephone to call a friend, but when you know how to keep your calls short so others can have access to the phone.

> MATURITY DOESN'T COME WITH AGE; IT COMES WITH AC- CEPTANCE OF RE- SPONSIBILITY.
> ED COLE

• Maturity is when you not only are old enough to stay at home alone, but when you can be trusted to stay at home and even have friends over.

• Maturity is when you are not only old enough to drive the car by yourself, but you pay for the gasoline you use.

• Maturity is when you are not only old enough to stay up late, but you are wise enough to go to bed early.

The more you learn to accept responsibility for your life, the more you will grow in maturity. With greater responsibility and maturity come greater privileges.

WHEN I WAS A CHILD, I SPOKE AS A CHILD, I UNDERSTOOD AS A CHILD, I THOUGHT AS A CHILD; BUT WHEN I BECAME A MAN, I PUT AWAY CHILDISH THINGS.

1 CORINTHIANS 13:11 NKJV

WISE WORDS

It can be said without qualification that no human being can consider himself mature if he narrows the use of his efforts, talents, or means to his own personal advantage. The very concept of maturity rests on the degree of inner growth that is characterized by a yearning within the individual to transcend his self-concentration by extending himself into the lives of others. In other words, maturity is a stage in his development, when to live with himself in a satisfying manner it becomes imperative for him to give as well as to receive.

ALVIN GOESER

ENCOURAGE
the young men
to be self–controlled.

TITUS 2:6 NIV

CAN YOU LOOK YOURSELF IN THE EYE?

WHEN YOU GET WHAT you want in your struggle for self,
And the world makes you king for a day,
Just go to a mirror and look at yourself,
And see what that man has to say.
For it isn't your father or mother or wife,
Whose judgment upon you must pass;
The fellow whose verdict counts most in your life,
Is the one staring back from the glass.
Some people may think you're a straight-shooting chum,
And call you a wonderful guy,
But the man in the glass says you're only a bum,
If you can't look him straight in the eye.
He's the fellow to please, never mind all the rest,
For he's with you clear up to the end,
And you have passed your most dangerous, difficult test,
If the man in the glass is your friend.
You may fool the whole world down your pathway of years,
And get pats on the back as you pass,
But your final reward will be heartache and tears,
If you've cheated the man in the glass.
—Anonymous

Learn to conquer yourself by developing your self-control, and you'll be able to look yourself straight in the eye and know you've done your best.

Who's Who: *Stephen L. Carter*

According to Stephen L. Carter, professor of Law at Yale University, integrity requires three central elements:
1. Discerning what is right and what is wrong.
2. Acting on what you have discerned, even at personal cost.
3. Saying openly that you are acting on your understanding of right from wrong.
Professor Carter explains:

Number one, discerning, requires that we reflect on the morality of our everyday choices.

Number two, acting on what we have discerned proves that we can trust ourselves to do what is right, even when it costs us something.

The third criteria underscores that a person of integrity is unashamed to declare personal beliefs of what is true, right, and good, while tempering these beliefs with compassion.

booklist

read more about it...prayer

- **131 Christians Everyone Should Know**
  by Mark Galli, Ted Olsen

- **The 7 Habits of Highly Effective Teens: The Ultimate Teenage Success Guide**
  by Sean Covey

- **Overcoming Obstacles to Reach Your Goals: Life Lessons from a Teen Entrepreneur**
  by D. J. Hanna

- **The Hiding Place**
  by Corrie ten Boom with John and Elizabeth Sherrill

- **More Christian Than African American**
  by Kimberly Cash Tate

GOD NEVER DISAPPOINTS

MARIAN HAD HER SIGHTS set on becoming a concert singer, a challenge that was doubly difficult because of the color of her skin. Her mother, however, had a patient trust in God. Marian later said, "Mother's religion made her believe that she would receive what was right for her to have if she was conscientious in her faith. If it did not come, it was because He had not considered it right for her. We grew in this atmosphere of faith that she created. . . . We believed as she did because we wanted the same kind of haven in the time of storm."

When Marian was denied admission to a famous music conservatory on account of her race, her mother calmly said that "someone would be raised up" to help her accomplish what she had hoped to do at the conservatory. That someone arrived only a few weeks later. One of Philadelphia's most outstanding voice teachers, Guiseppe Boghetti, made room for her to become one of his students.

Marian Anderson was on her way to becoming one of the most magnificent singers of the twentieth century. On Easter Sunday in 1939, she sang for more than 75,000 people gathered in front of the Lincoln Memorial and gave a performance never forgotten by those who were there. Trusting her future to God, she accomplished more than she could have dreamed.

Regardless of the opposition you encounter in reaching your dream, always remember that God is on your side.

> **Trust In** yourself and you are doomed to disappointment; but trust in God, and you are never to be confounded in time or eternity.
>
> DWIGHT L. MOODY

It is better to take refuge in the Lord than to trust in man.

PSALM 118:8 NIV

CONSIDER THIS!

The Chinese character for the word "integrity" is a combination of the characters that represent the word *person* and the word *word*. Something like this:

Person + Word = Integrity

The Chinese find it incomprehensible that a person of integrity would fail to keep his or her word. That's a good lesson for us in the western world, where we depend on contracts and litigation to keep things just and fair. As Christians, we too should find it unacceptable to say one thing and do another. Shouldn't God be able to count on us to keep our word, especially when He has always kept His?

GOD'S FAVOR RESTS ON THOSE WHO KEEP THEIR WORD

In *Up from Slavery,* Booker T. Washington describes meeting an ex-slave from Virginia:

> **A GOOD REPUTATION IS MORE VALUABLE THAN MONEY.**
>
> PUBLILIUS SYRUS

"I found that this man had made a contract with his master, two or three years previous to the Emancipation Proclamation, to the effect that the slave was to be permitted to buy himself, by paying so much per year for his body; and while he was paying for himself, he was to be permitted to labor where and for whom he pleased.

"Finding that he could secure better wages in Ohio, he went there. When freedom came, he was still in debt to his master some 300 dollars. Notwithstanding that the Emancipation Proclamation freed him from any obligation to his master, this black man walked the greater portion of the distance back to where his old master lived in Virginia, and placed the last dollar, with interest, in his hands.

"In talking to me about this, the man told me that he knew that he did not have to pay his debt, but that he had given his word to his master, and his word he had never broken. He felt that he could not enjoy his freedom till he had fulfilled his promise."

Your ability to keep your word, not your ability to acquire money, is your true measure as a person!

Choose a good reputation over great riches.

PROVERBS 22:1 NLT

CHOOSING FRIENDS WISELY

A missionary surgeon in one of China's hospitals restored sight to a man who had been nearly blinded by cataracts. A few weeks later, to his great surprise, forty-eight blind men showed up on his hospital's doorstep. They had all come to be cured. Amazingly, these blind men had walked more than 250 miles from a remote area of China to get to the hospital. They had traveled by holding on to a rope chain. Their guide and inspiration was the man who had been cured.

> **As iron** sharpens iron, a friend sharpens a friend.
>
> PROVERBS 27:17 NLT

The Christian evangelist, Dr. J. Wilbur Chapman, concluded from his study of the New Testament Gospels that Jesus healed some forty people personally and directly. Of this number, thirty-four were brought to Him by friends or family members, or Jesus was taken to the ailing person by others. Only six of the forty people healed in the Gospels found their way to Jesus, or He to them, without someone giving assistance.

In the Gospels, Jesus refers to His followers as "friends." To them, He was the Friend of friends, closer even than a brother. Not only do you become like the friends with whom you associate, but when you choose to hang out with friends who are like Jesus, you will find yourself imitating Him more and more.

Keep company with good men and good men you will imitate.

#1 **If you desire to choose the right kind of friends—those who will have a positive influence on you, try these helpful suggestions:**

#2 1. Choose friends who share your belief in God.

2. Choose friends who share similar values.

3. Choose friends with integrity.

#3 4. Choose friends who are kind.

5. Choose friends you might approve of for your little brother or sister.

#4

#5

#6

#7

#8

Facts

Fun

• Guess who combined two previously unrelated inventions to invent something completely different? One day Johann Gutenberg began toying with the notion of using the wine press and the coin punch to imprint paper. His idea gave birth to the printing press.

• Guess who came up with the idea for the office staple "Liquid Paper"? Former "Monkee" Mike Nesmith had a rather creative mother, Bette Nesmith Graham. Her invention—liquid paper—was initially rejected by IBM, but that didn't stop her. She came up with a way to make and market the product herself.

• Guess who invented the ever-popular board game Monopoly? Inventor Clarence Darrow presented the game to Parker Bros., but they rejected it, saying it had too many fundamental playing errors. Darrow believed his game would be a winner, so he decided to produce it himself. When the game became a hit with consumers, Parker Bros. finally came on board.

KEEP AT IT

The **way** to get to the **top**
is to get **off** your **bottom**.

Dr. Eugene Swearingen

One day, in the fall of 1894, Guglielmo retreated to his room on the third floor of his parents' home. He had just spent his entire summer vacation reading books and filling notebooks with squiggly diagrams. Now the time had come to work.

He rose early every morning. He worked all day and long into the night, to the point that his mother became alarmed. He had never been a robust person, but now he was appallingly thin. His face was drawn, and his eyes were often glazed over with fatigue.

Finally, the day came when he announced his instruments were ready. He invited the family to his room, and pushing a button, he succeeded in ringing a bell on the first floor! While his mother was amazed, his father was not. He saw no use in being able to send a signal so short a distance. So Guglielmo labored on. Little by little, he made changes in his invention, so he could send a signal from one hill to the next and then beyond the hill. Eventually, his invention was perfected, partly by inspiration but mostly by perseverance.

Guglielmo Marconi eventually was hailed as the inventor of wireless telegraphy—the forerunner of the radio. He not only received a Nobel Prize in physics for his efforts, but also a seat in the Italian senate and many honorary degrees and titles.

You can accomplish anything you set your heart on by combining your vision with hard work.

How long will you lie down, O sluggard?
When will you arise from your sleep?

PROVERBS 6:9 NASB

CORRECT YOUR MISTAKES

A janitor at the First Security Bank in Boise, Idaho, once accidentally put a box of eight thousand checks worth $840,000 on a trash table. That night, the operator of the paper shredder dutifully dumped the box of checks into his machine, which cut the checks into quarter-inch shreds. He then dumped the paper scraps into a garbage can outside the bank. When the bank supervisor realized what happened the next morning, he wanted to cry.

Most of the checks had been cashed at the bank and were awaiting shipment to a clearinghouse. Their loss represented a bookkeeping nightmare since most of the checks were still unrecorded, and as a result, the bankers could not know who paid what to whom.

> AN ERROR DOESN'T BECOME A MISTAKE UNTIL YOU REFUSE TO CORRECT IT.
>
> ORLANDO A. BATTISTA

What did the supervisor do? He ordered that the shredded pieces be reconstructed. Fifty employees worked in two shifts for six hours a day inside six rooms—shifting, matching, and pasting the pieces together as if they were jigsaw puzzles—until all eight thousand of the checks were put together again.

Humpty Dumpty may have fallen from the wall, but did the king's men even try to put him together again? If you make a mistake, work on a solution!

HE WHO HEEDS DISCIPLINE SHOWS THE WAY TO LIFE, BUT WHOEVER IGNORES CORRECTION LEADS OTHERS ASTRAY.

PROVERBS 10:17 NIV

WISE WORDS

Never let mistakes or wrong directions, of which every man falls into many, discourage you. There is precious instruction to be got by finding where we were wrong.

THOMAS CARLYLE

STAND BY YOUR FRIENDS

> WE SHOULD BEHAVE TO OUR FRIENDS AS WE WOULD WISH OUR FRIENDS TO BEHAVE TO US.
>
> ARISTOTLE

PRESIDENT Harry Truman had a reputation for having never been sly or disloyal in his life. He stood by a friend even when he risked public ridicule for it.

One of Truman's friends from his army days was Jim Pendergast, whose Uncle Tom was the head of the Democratic Party in Kansas City. Jim and his dad urged Truman to run for office—a judgeship in rural Jackson County. A year later Truman did so, and with Pendergast's support, he won the election. As judge, he didn't always agree with Pendergast's practices. Tom once said to a group of contractors who had asked him to influence Truman, "I told you he was the hardheadedest, orneriest man in the world; there isn't anything I can do."

Unfortunately, Pendergast's penchant for horse races caused him to be investigated for income tax evasion. He confessed, was fined, and was sentenced to serve fifteen months in a federal penitentiary. When Pendergast died during Truman's vice-presidency, Truman didn't hesitate to fly to Kansas City for the funeral. "He was always my friend," Truman said of him, "and I have always been his."

True friendship is not based on what a friend does for you, but on what he means to you.

Do to others as you would have them do to you.

LUKE 6:31 NIV

TOP **10** TIPS for Building Strong Friendships

1. FORGIVE OFFENSES QUICKLY.
2. REMAIN LOYAL.
3. INVEST YOURSELF.
4. END DISAGREEMENTS.
5. RESPECT YOUR DIFFERENCES.
6. DEVELOP MUTUAL INTERESTS.
7. SHOW KINDNESS.
8. HAVE COMPASSION.
9. INITIATE POSITIVE INFLUENCE.
10. PROMOTE FAITH, HOPE, AND LOVE.

HOW Do YOU MEASURE Up?

Is your life attitude passive or proactive?

When I'm introduced to someone I find attractive, do I:
   A. Shy away after a muffled "hello?"
   B. Tell myself that someone this attractive could never be interested in me?
   C. Ask interested questions about this person's life?

When my mom tells me there is a "help wanted" sign in the window of the corner store, I:
   A. Clean up, put on my best clothes, and stop by the next day to talk to the manager.
   B. Wait a few days, then call the store about the opening.
   C. Tell myself no one will hire me anyway; there's no point in following up.
   D. Blow it off completely. My mom doesn't know what's up.

Don't let your life slip through your fingers. Ask God to help you turn the negative attitudes in your life into positive ones.

TAKE THE FIRST STEP

DON'T BE DISCOURAGED; EVERYONE WHO GOT WHERE HE IS, STARTED WHERE HE WAS.

During the late 1960s, a couple was vacationing in the California mountains one day, and they noticed a pleasant-appearing young man sitting by a bridge near their hotel. Day after day they saw him sitting in that same spot. At first, they assumed he was fishing, but after taking a closer look, they realized he was doing nothing—just sitting and staring into space. Finally, on the last day of their vacation, they couldn't stand it anymore. They just had to ask: "Why do you sit in that one spot all day, every day?"

He replied with a smile, "I happen to believe in reincarnation. I believe that I have lived many times before and that I will have many lives following this one. So this life I'm sitting out."

In reality, it's impossible for any of us to sit out life. Each day, we are either moving forward or backward, getting stronger or weaker, moving higher or lower. Each of us begins every new day with a fresh opportunity to change tomorrow's starting point.

You only have one chance at it. What will you do today to make your tomorrow better?

Though your beginning was insignificant,
Yet your end will increase greatly.

JOB 8:7 NASB

CONSIDER THIS!

Consider these insights about flattery:

- Flattery corrupts both the receiver and the giver.
  Edmund Burke

- I can't be your friend, and your flatterer too.
  Thomas Fuller

- Flattery is a false coinage, which our vanity puts
  into circulation.
  La Rouchefoucauld

- We do not hate flattery, any one of us—we all like it.
  Charles H. Spurgeon

- Among all the diseases of the mind there is not one
  more pernicious than the love of flattery.
  Richard Steel

- Flattery is the worst and falsest way of showing our
  esteem.
  Jonathan Swift

FLATTERY WILL GET YOU SOMEWHERE

In ancient Greece, the philosopher Aristippus considered by all who knew him to be the master of political craftiness—learned to get along well in royal circles by flattering the tyrant Denys. Not only did he flatter Denys, but he was proud that he did. In fact, Aristippus disdained less prosperous fellow philosophers and wise men who refused to stoop that low.

One day, Aristippus saw his colleague Diogenes washing vegetables, and he said to him, "If you would only learn to flatter King Denys, you would not have to be washing lentils." Diogenes looked up slowly and replied,

> TREAT EVERYBODY ALIKE, NO MATTER FROM WHAT STATION IN LIFE HE COMES. . . . REALLY GREAT MEN AND WOMEN ARE THOSE WHO ARE NATURAL, FRANK, AND HONEST WITH EVERYONE WITH WHOM THEY COME INTO CONTACT.
> WILLIAM H. DANFORTH

"And you, if you had only learned to live on lentils, would not have to flatter King Denys."

Another way to regard flattery is this:

F—foolish
L—laughable
A—accolades
T—to
T—tell
E—everyone
R—'round
Y—you

Speak the truth sincerely. When the truth is painful, consider the option of remaining silent!

Don't show favoritism.

JAMES 2:1 NIV

SWEET RELEASE

LLOYD JOHN OGILVIE wrote in *Let God Love You,* "The hardest time to be gentle is when we know we are right and someone else is obviously dead wrong. . . . But the greatest temptation for most of us is when someone has failed us and has admitted it, and their destiny or happiness is in our hands. We hold the power to give or refuse a blessing.

"Recently, a dear friend hurt me in both word and action. Each time we met . . . I almost began to enjoy the leverage of being the offended one. His first overtures of restitution were resisted because of the gravity of the judgment I had made. He had taken a key idea I had shared with him in confidence and had developed it as his own before I had a chance to use it. The plagiarism of ideas had been coupled with the use of some of my written material, reproduced under his name. . . . The most difficult thing was to surrender my indignation and work through my hurt. . . .

"Finally, the Lord got me where He wanted me. . . . His word to me was clear and undeniable; 'Lloyd, why is it so important to you who gets the credit, just so My work gets done?' I gave up my right to be what only God could be as this man's judge and savior. The gentle attitude began to flow."

When we withhold forgiveness, it not only hurts the person we don't want to forgive, it hurts us. Our creativity and joy in life are stifled. When we forgive, we release peace and restoration to the forgiven and to ourselves.

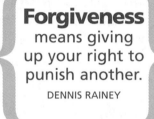

Forgiveness means giving up your right to punish another.

DENNIS RAINEY

Jesus said, "When you stand praying, if you hold anything against anyone, forgive him, so that your Father in heaven may forgive you your sins."

MARK 11:25 NIV

A while back, my best friend did something that hurt my feelings really badly. He said he was sorry, and I said I forgave him, but I find that the resentment creeps back in when I least expect it, and I have to forgive all over again. How can I let go of it and put it behind me?

Forgiveness is a choice—a moment in time when we decide to forgive a wrong done to us. Most people understand that part. The problem is that forgiveness has two parts. It is also a process. This is the part that most people overlook and the part that's giving you some trouble. It takes time and hard work to get past the hurt and disappointment caused by a betrayal. The good news is that it's doable.

Think of it this way. A tornado goes through your town and damages your home. If that happened, your parents would have to make the decision to move you all to another place or try to repair or rebuild your home. If they decide to stay, it will take time before things can be back to normal—and frankly, the new or restored home will always be a little different from the original.

You've taken the first step and decided to rebuild your relationship with your friend. Now give it time. Build new good memories to replace the old, painful ones. Every morning, thank God for your friend and consciously count off the things you like about him. Before long your head will be dancing with your heart once again.

booklist

read more about it...humor

- *Snickers from the Front Pew*
  by Todd and Jedd Hafer
- *Laughter from Heaven*
  by Barbara Johnson
- *Live Long and Die Laughing*
  by Mark Lowry
- *Laughing Out Loud*
  Compiled by Rebecca Currington

A GOOD SENSE OF HUMOR

A MISSIONARY FROM Sweden was once urged by his friends to give up his idea of returning to India because it was so hot there. "Man," the fellow Swede urged, as if telling his friend something he didn't already know, "it's 120 degrees in the shade in that country!" The Swedish missionary replied "Vell, ve don't alvays have to stay in the shade do ve?"

Humor is not a sin. It is a God-given escape hatch. Being able to see the lighter side of life is a virtue. Every vocation and circumstance of life has a lighter side, if we are only willing to see it. Wholesome humor can do a great deal to help defuse a tense, heated situation. In developing a good sense of humor, we must be able to laugh at our own mistakes; accept justified criticism and recover from it; and learn to avoid using statements that are unsuitable, even though they may be funny.

> **Laughter** is the sun that drives winter from the human face.
> VICTOR HUGO

James M. Gray and William Houghton—two Godly men—were praying together one day, and the elderly Dr. Gray concluded his prayer by saying, "Lord, keep me cheerful. Keep me from becoming a cranky, old man."

Keeping a sense of humor is a great way to become a sweet, patient, and encouraging person. Learn to laugh at yourself occasionally!

A cheerful heart brings a smile to your face; a sad heart makes it hard to get through the day.

PROVERBS 15:13 MSG

Under [Christ's] direction the whole BODY is fitted together perfectly, and each part in its OWN special way helps the other parts.

EPHESIANS 4:16 TLB

> **I am only one; but still I am one. I cannot do everything, but still I can do something; I will not refuse to do the something I can do.**
>
> **Helen Keller**

YOU CAN MAKE A DIFFERENCE

JEWISH PHYSICIAN BORIS Kornfeld was imprisoned in Siberia. There he worked in surgery, helping both the staff and prisoners. He met a Christian whose name is unknown, but whose quiet faith and frequent reciting of the Lord's Prayer had an impact on Dr. Kornfeld.

One day while repairing the slashed artery of a guard, Dr. Kornfeld seriously considered suturing the artery in such a way that the guard would slowly die of internal bleeding. The violence he recognized in his own heart appalled him, and he found himself saying, "Forgive us our sins as we forgive those who sin against us." Afterward, he began to refuse to obey various inhumane, immoral, prison-camp rules. He knew his quiet rebellion put his life in danger.

One afternoon, he examined a patient who had undergone an operation to remove cancer. He saw in the man's eyes a depth of spiritual misery that moved him with compassion, and he told him his entire story, including a confession of his secret faith. That very night, Dr. Kornfeld was murdered as he slept, but his testimony was not in vain.

The patient who had heard his confession became a Christian as a result. He survived the prison camp and went on to tell the world about life in the gulag.

That patient was Aleksandr Solzhenitsyn, who became one of the leading Russian writers of the twentieth century. He revealed to the world the horrors of the prison camps and perils of Russian communism. One person can truly make a difference. There is something you can do, and only you can do it. God created you with a destiny.

Who's Who:

Marcia Bullard

As President, CEO and editor of *USA Weekend*, 47-year-old Marcia Bullard didn't need a new cause to prove her success. But she wanted to do more.

In 1992, Bullard had an idea. Since it was leap year, she suggested that people use the extra day to do something kind for their neighbors. More than 70,000 people listened and acted, and "Make a Difference Day" was born.

Now the biggest day of volunteering in the country, Bullard's call to compassion has significantly changed the world around her.

Marcia Bullard was simply reaching out to others and she started a movement that is changing the world. Is there an idea that God has planted in your heart? It may seem small, even insignificant. But don't be too hasty to disregard it.

FIND WAYS
TO BENEFIT OTHERS

This American received a medical degree from New York University College of Medicine. He received an appointment to the Virus Research Laboratory at the University of Pittsburgh. He received an assignment from the army to develop a vaccine against influenza, and among the many honors he received was a Presidential Medal of Freedom.

Jonas Salk, however, is not known for what he received, but for what he gave. He and his team of researchers gave their efforts to prepare an inactivated polio virus that could serve as an immunizing agent against polio. By 1952, they had created a vaccine; and in 1955, the vaccine was released for widespread use in the United States, virtually ending the ravaging, crippling effects of polio.

> NO PERSON WAS EVER HONORED FOR WHAT HE RECEIVED. HONOR HAS BEEN THE REWARD FOR WHAT HE GAVE.
>
> CALVIN COOLIDGE

You will receive many opportunities in your life and, most likely, a number of certificates, diplomas, and awards. What ultimately will count, however, is what you do with the training you have received and the skills and traits you have developed.

Find a way to give, create, or generate something today that will benefit others. In your actions will be not only a potential for fame and reward, but also great personal satisfaction—the reward of highest value.

THE RIGHTEOUS GIVE WITHOUT SPARING.

PROVERBS 21:26 NIV

WISE WORDS

Christ has no body now on earth but yours;
Yours are the only hands with which he can
    do his work,
Yours are the only feet with which he can
    go about the world,
Yours are the only eyes through which his
    compassion can shine forth upon a
    troubled world.
Christ has no body now on earth but yours.

TERESA OF AVILA

Fun Facts

How good are you at finding the right word? Try these:

1. The speeding car (A) collided with (B) crashed into the telephone pole.
2. The four-car accident (A) occurred (B) took place on a foggy section of the interstate.
3. Only 12 (A) people (B) persons joined the Latin club at school this year.
4. Cindy promised to (A) lend (B) loan me her car while mine is in the shop.

ANSWERS:
1: (B) crashed into. Both objects have to be moving in order to collide.
2. (A) occurred. Use take only to refer to something that has been scheduled.
3. (A) people. In the case of person, two's a crowd. If you have more than one person, you have people. It's a simple rule that will help you avoid unnecessarily complicated decisions.
4. (A) lend. Lend is a verb meaning "allow to borrow." Loan is used as a verb in the context of a financial transaction.

THINK BEFORE YOU SPEAK

The **difference** between the **right** word and the almost **right** word is the **difference** between lightning and the lightning bug.

MARK TWAIN

Consider the infamous statements listed below, and notice as you read that they all could be corrected by changing or inserting only one word!

"Everything that can be invented has been invented."
—Charles H. Duell, U.S. Patent Office director, 1899

"Who wants to hear actors talk?"
—H.M. Warner, Warner Brothers Pictures, 1927

"There is no likelihood man can ever tap the power of the atom."
—Robert Millikan, Nobel Prize winner in physics, 1923

"Sensible and responsible women do not want to vote."
—Grover Cleveland, 1905

"Heavier-than-air flying machines are impossible."
—Lord Kelvin, president, Royal Society, 1895

"[Babe] Ruth made a big mistake when he gave up pitching."
—Tris Speaker, 1927

"*Gone with the Wind* is going to be the biggest flop in Hollywood history."
—Gary Cooper

Isn't it amazing what a difference a word or two can make! Choose your words carefully. Always think before you speak.

The right word at the right time is like a custom-made piece of jewelry.

PROVERBS 25:11 MSG

PREPARING FOR SPIRITUAL COMBAT

TEMPTATION CAN CAUSE US TO SUCCUMB, SINK, SIN, OR STAND.

WILLIAM A. WARD

WE CAN LEARN a great deal from the Alaskan bull moose. Each fall, during the breeding season, the males of the species battle for dominance. They literally go head-to-head, antlers crunching together as they collide. When antlers are broken, defeat is ensured since a moose's antlers are its only weapon.

Generally speaking, the heftiest moose with the largest and strongest antlers wins. Therefore, the battle is nearly always predetermined the summer before. It is then that the moose eat nearly 'round the clock. The one that consumes the best diet for growing antlers and gaining weight will be the victor. Those who eat inadequately will have weaker antlers and less bulk. The fight itself involves far more brawn than brain and more reliance on bulk than on skill.

What is the lesson for us? Spiritual battles are inevitable. We each experience seasons of attack in our lives. Whether we are the victors or the victims depends not on our skills or brainpower but on our spiritual strength. What we do in advance of the war determines the outcome of the battle. Now is the time to develop enduring faith, strength, and wisdom. Now is the time for prayer, reading, and memorizing God's Word. Then, when the opportunity comes, you'll be prepared.

Take up the whole armor of God, that you may be able to withstand in the evil day, and having done all, to stand.

EPHESIANS 6:13 NKJV

TOP **10** TIPS on How to Prepare for Spiritual Warfare

1. PRAY FOR STRENGTH.

2. READ YOUR BIBLE.

3. COMMIT SCRIPTURES TO MEMORY.

4. HAVE FAITH IN GOD'S SPIRIT TO GUIDE YOU.

5. ASK A FRIEND TO PRAY WITH YOU.

6. NURTURE A HEART OF GRATITUDE.

7. PUT YOURSELF IN GOD'S HANDS.

8. WORSHIP EVERY DAY.

9. REMEMBER THAT THE BATTLE IS THE LORD'S.

10. REALIZE GOD IS IN CONTROL AND THROW YOURSELF ON HIS MERCY AND GRACE.

HOW Do YOU MEASURE Up?

How do you respond when you are in a group of people who are talking badly about a friend?

A. I get up and leave.
B. I say that I feel uncomfortable with the conversation.
C. I defend my friend.
D. I get angry and remain silent.

How do you respond when a friend tells you a rumor about another friend?

A. I remain silent. I don't want to offend anyone.
B. I participate in the conversation. It's fun.
C. I tell my friend that people are talking about her or him.
D. I pray for my friends.

If your honest response is not one you can be proud of, ask God to help you become the friend you should be.

A FRIEND IS A FRIEND AT ALL TIMES

WHO CEASES TO BE A FRIEND, NEVER WAS ONE.

In *Lessons from Mom,* Joan Aho Ryan writes about loyalty in friendship. She says, "We went to one of the local shopping malls recently where Mom ran into two women who live in her development. . . . They greeted her effusively. It was a brief exchange, during which she introduced me, and they were on their way. 'What phony baloney,' she said when they were well ahead of us. Since her remark came from nowhere, I asked her what she meant.

"With obvious disdain, she explained that she had sat under the canopy at her pool on several occasions with these two women and one of their friends, Sylvia. One day, she said, she sat nearby and heard the three of them talking about the wedding reception of Sylvia's daughter the week before. They raved about the food, the flowers, the elegant country club location, the beautiful bride. . . . Mom said Sylvia was obviously beaming with pride.

"'Well, then Sylvia left, and you should have heard them,' Mom said. . . . 'I couldn't believe friends could be that two-faced. They ripped her apart, talking about how cheap she was, her homely son-in-law, the music they couldn't dance to. It was awful. And they call themselves friends,' she clucked. 'Who needs friends like that?'"

Speaking well of others is not only a good way to acquire friends, but to keep them.

A friend loves at all times.

PROVERBS 17:17 NIV

IF YOU DON'T HAVE ANYTHING TO SAY, DON'T TALK!

Albert Einstein is reputed to have had a wholesome disregard for the tyranny of custom. One evening, the president of Swarthmore College hosted a dinner held in Einstein's honor. Although he was not scheduled to speak during the event—only to receive an award—after the award was made, the audience clamored, "Speech, speech!" The president turned the podium over to him. Einstein reluctantly came forward and said only this: "Ladies and gentlemen, I am very sorry but I have nothing to say." And then he sat down.

A few seconds later, he stood back up and said, "In case I do have something to say, I'll come back."

Some six months later, Einstein wired the president of the college with this message: "Now I have something to say."

Another dinner was held, and this time, Einstein made a speech.

If you have nothing to say, it's wise to say nothing. If you do have something to say, it's wise to say it in as few words as possible. As the old saying goes, "If your mind should go blank, don't forget to turn off the sound."

> **The more** talk, the less truth; the wise measure their words.
>
> PROVERBS 10:19 MSG

The most valuable of all talents is that of never using two words when one will do.

THOMAS JEFFERSON

☑ JUST DO IT

#1 **If you find you are talking more than you should, try these helpful tips:**

1. Ask others thoughtful questions about themselves.
2. Practice listening skills.
3. Nod and smile to show interest instead of talking.
4. Make eye contact to affirm your attention instead of talking.
5. Introduce others into the conversation.

#2

#3

#4

#5

#6

#7

#8

#9

#10

CONSIDER THIS!

Norman Vincent Peale was often asked, "Don't you think life would be better if we had fewer problems?" He always answered the same way. "I'll be happy to take you to Woodlawn Cemetery because the only people I know who don't have any problems are dead."

Dr. Peale even believed that problems were useful. They make us feel alive. They help us to depend on God and stay in fellowship with Him. He once said, "If you have no problems at all, you're in grave jeopardy! I suggest you race home, go straight to your bedroom, and slam the door. Then get down on your knees and pray: "What's the matter, Lord? Don't You trust me anymore? Give me some problems!"

Peale had a remarkable attitude toward problems. He felt the solution was in the attitude. He encouraged people to think of problems as opportunities. He believed in the power of positive thinking.

How do you deal with problems?

MAKE THE MOST OF YOUR SITUATION

A story is told of identical twins: one a hope-filled optimist who often said, "Everything is coming up roses!" and the other, a sad and hopeless pessimist who continually expected the worst to happen. The concerned parents of the twins took them to a psychologist, hoping he might be able to help them balance their personalities.

The psychologist suggested that on the twins' next birthday, the parents put them in separate rooms to open their gifts. "Give the pessimist the best toys you can afford," the psychologist said, "and give the optimist a box of manure." The parents did as he said.

THE HAPPIEST PEOPLE DON'T NECESSARILY HAVE THE BEST OF EVERYTHING. THEY JUST MAKE THE BEST OF EVERYTHING.

When they peeked in on the pessimistic twin, they heard him complaining, "I don't like the color of this toy. I'll bet this toy will break! I don't like to play this game. I know someone who has a bigger toy than this!"

Tiptoeing across the corridor, the parents peeked in and saw their optimistic son gleefully throwing manure up in the air. He was giggling as he said, "You can't fool me! Where there's this much manure, there's gotta be a pony!"

How are you looking at life today? As an accident waiting to happen or a blessing about to be received?

Not that I speak in regard to need,
for I have learned in whatever state I am,
to be content: . . . I can do all things through
Christ who strengthens me.

PHILIPPIANS 4:11,13 NKJV

WORDS MAKE A DIFFERENCE

One day, a young altar boy was serving the priest at a Sunday Mass being held in the country church of his small village. The boy, nervous in his new role at the altar, accidentally dropped the cruet of wine. The village priest immediately struck the boy sharply on the cheek and in a very gruff voice, shouted so that many people could hear, "Leave the altar and don't come back!" That boy became Tito, the Communist leader who ruled Yugoslavia for many decades.

One day in a large city cathedral, a young boy was serving a bishop at a Sunday Mass. He, too, accidentally dropped the cruet of wine. The bishop turned to him but rather than responding in anger, gently whispered with a warm twinkle in his eyes, "Someday you will be a priest." That boy grew up to become Archbishop Fulton Sheen.

> DO NOT REMOVE A FLY FROM YOUR FORE-HEAD WITH A HATCHET.
> CHINESE PROVERB

Words have power. The childhood phrase, "Sticks and stones can break my bones, but words can never hurt me," simply isn't true. Words do hurt. They wound—sometimes deeply.

Words also can reward, build self-esteem, create friendships, give hope, and render a blessing. Words can heal and drive accomplishment.

Watch what you say to a friend today! Are your words like poison to the heart, or do they drip with the sweetness of honey?

REPROVE, REBUKE, EXHORT, WITH GREAT PATIENCE AND INSTRUCTION.

2 TIMOTHY 4:2 NASB

WISE WORDS

If you found a person whose speech was perfectly true, you'd have a perfect person, in perfect control of life. A bit in the mouth of a horse controls the whole horse. A small rudder on a huge ship in the hand of a skilled captain sets a course in the face of the strongest winds. A word out of your mouth may seem of no account, but it can accomplish nearly anything—or destroy it! It only takes a spark, remember, to set off a forest fire. A careless or wrongly placed word out of your mouth can do that.

JAMES 3:2-5 MSG

booklist

read more about it...
motivation and inspiration

- *Teens Can Make It Happen Workbook*
  by Stedman Graham

- *The 7 Habits of Highly Effective Teens*
  by Sean Covey

- *Reach for Your Dreams*
  by White Stone Books

- *Checklist for Life for Teens*
  by Thomas Nelson

YOU ARE AWESOME, CREATED IN GOD'S IMAGE

A FARMER ONCE , a young eagle in the forest, brought it home, and raised it among his ducks and turkeys. Five years later, a naturalist came to visit him and saw the bird. "That's an eagle not a chicken!" he said. "Yes," said the farmer, "but I've raised it to be a chicken." "Still," said the naturalist, "it has a wingspan of fifteen feet. It's an eagle!" "It will never fly," said the farmer. The naturalist disagreed, and they decided to put their argument to the test.

First, the naturalist picked up the eagle and said, "Eagle, thou art an eagle; thou dost belong to the sky and not to this earth; stretch forth thy wings and fly." The eagle saw the chickens and jumped down. The next day, the naturalist took the eagle to the top of the house and said the same thing before letting the eagle go. Again, it spotted the chickens below and fluttered down to join them in feeding.

"One more try," said the naturalist. He took the eagle up a mountain. The trembling bird looked around, and then the naturalist made it look into the sun. Suddenly, the eagle stretched out its wings, gave a mighty screech, and flew away, never to return.

People may say you are just a hunk of flesh—a chicken rather than an eagle. But deep inside, you have a spirit created in God's image, and you are destined to fly.

> **Every Calling** is great when greatly pursued.
>
> Oliver Wendell Holmes

I press toward the goal for the prize of the upward call of God in Christ Jesus.

PHILIPPIANS 3:14 NKJV

JESUS IS YOUR PATH

E. STANLEY JONES TELLS the story of a missionary who became lost in an African jungle. Looking around, he saw nothing but bush and a few clearings. He stumbled about until he finally came across a native hut. He asked one of the natives if he could lead him out of the jungle and back to the mission station. The native agreed to help him.

"Thank you!" exclaimed the missionary. "Which way do I go?" The native replied, "Walk." And so they did, hacking their way through the unmarked jungle for more than an hour.

In pausing to rest, the missionary looked around and had the same overwhelming sense that he was lost. Again, all he could see was bush and a few clearings. "Are you quite sure this is the way?" he asked. "I don't see any path."

The native looked at him and replied, "Bwana, in this place there is no path. I am the path."

When we have no clues about which direction we're going, we must remember that God who guides us is omniscient—all-wise. When we run out of time, we must remember that God is omnipresent—all time is in His hand. When we are weak, we must remember that God is omnipotent—all-powerful. He is everything we need.

> **It is** impossible for that man to despair who remembers that his Helper is omnipotent.
>
> JEREMY TAYLOR

I will lift up my eyes to the mountains; from where shall my help come? My help comes from the Lord, who made heaven and earth.

PSALM 121:1-2 NASB

new insights into ageless questions

I gave my life to the Lord when I was just a child, but sometimes I don't feel saved; in fact, I feel lost. What can I do to wash away my doubts and be able to rest securely knowing that I'm going to heaven when I die?

What you are describing is common—we all have doubts sometimes. Fortunately, our salvation does not depend on our feelings. It is a fact that we can rely upon. We have been given the gift of salvation through Jesus Christ. That's an unshakable truth, supported by God's Word—the Bible. (Read Romans 10:9-10; Acts 10:43; Isaiah 45:22.)

On days when your feelings don't match that fact, rest in the assurance of your salvation—that's faith, believing in something you don't see or feel. Have faith and let your faith grow through times of doubt. And don't worry, the feelings will come, the assurance will come, the joy will come as you spend time with your Heavenly Father and keep your faith securely anchored to Him.

Fun Facts

Next fall when you see geese flying south in a V formation, you might be interested in what science has discovered about their behavior.

As each bird flaps its wings, it creates an updraft for the bird immediately following it. By flying in a V formation, the whole flock adds at least 71 percent greater flying range than if each bird flew on its own.

Whenever a goose falls out of formation, it suddenly feels the drag and resistance of trying to go it alone and quickly gets back into formation to take advantage of the lifting power of the bird immediately in front. When the lead goose gets tired, it rotates back in the V and another bird takes the point position. The geese honk from behind to encourage those up front to keep up their speed.

Finally, when a goose gets sick or is wounded by gun shots and falls out, two geese fall out of formation and follow it down to help and protect it. They stay with the fallen bird until it is either able to fly or it dies. Then and only then do they launch out on their own or with another formation to catch up with their group.

REAL FRIENDS WANT WHAT'S BEST FOR YOU

'Tis **better** to be **alone**, than in **bad company**.

GEORGE WASHINGTON

Coach Gregory watched with pride as Rashaan Salaam accepted the Heisman Trophy. He recalled the hotshot eighteen-year-old who, finally free from his mother's tight discipline, had arrived in Colorado ready to devour the world. He said, "Rashaan was a gangster wannabe. He came here wearing all this red stuff, talking about gangs. He hadn't done it back home because his mother would never have tolerated it." Neither did Gregory. He never lectured or preached to Rashaan, but he did ask him questions. When Rashaan came to him, talking about his new friends, Gregory said, "Sure, they are your friends, but are you their friend? They know what you're trying to accomplish. They know the potential you have to do great things. If you are their friend, when they get ready to get into something, they'll say, 'Salaam, get out of here. Go home and study.'"

As a coach, Gregory wanted Salaam to find daylight and get into the end zone; but as his friend, he wanted him to live in the daylight and make it to life's goal line as a productive citizen. Winning a football game is never a one-man effort. It's a team effort. The same holds true for life, and the good news is you can choose the players on your team!

Do not be misled: "Bad company corrupts good character."

1 CORINTHIANS 15:33 NIV

A LESSON FROM THE LOBSTER

LAZINESS IS OFTEN MISTAKEN FOR PATIENCE.

HENRY WARD Beecher, one of the most powerful preachers in American history, gave this illustration in one of his sermons:

"The lobster, when left high and dry among the rocks, has no sense and energy enough to work his way back to the sea, but waits for the sea to come to him. If it does not come, he remains where he is, and dies, although the slightest exertion would enable him to reach the waves, which are perhaps tossing and tumbling within a yard of him.

"There is a tide in human affairs that casts men into 'tight places,' and leaves them there, like stranded lobsters. If they choose to lie where the breakers have flung them, expecting some grand billow to take them on its big shoulders and carry them to smooth water, the chances are that their hopes will never be realized."

Laziness is doing nothing, hoping nothing, being nothing. Patience, on the other hand, doesn't mean not doing anything. It means working on in hope that what you're waiting for will eventually come to pass, but you will continue to work on even if it doesn't.

Let us lay aside every weight, and the sin which so easily ensnares us, and let us run with endurance the race that is set before us.

HEBREWS 12:1 NKJV

TOP 10 TIPS for Running the Race That Is Set Before Us

1. WRITE DOWN YOUR GOALS.

2. LIST YOUR PRIORITIES.

3. LIST STEPS TOWARD ACCOMPLISHING YOUR GOALS AND PRIORITIES.

4. START EACH DAY WITH A PRAYER AND AFFIRMATION.

5. KEEP HOPE STRONG IN YOUR HEART.

6. ASK GOD FOR HELP EACH DAY.

7. ACCOMPLISH THREE STEPS EACH WEEK ON YOUR TO-DO LIST.

8. ESTABLISH ACCOUNTABILITY WITH A TRUSTED FRIEND.

9. TELL YOUR PASTOR ABOUT YOUR GOALS.

10. JOURNAL YOUR SUCCESSES AS WELL AS YOUR MISTAKES.

CONSIDER THIS!

Wallace Fridy notes, "Old Faithful is not the largest geyser, nor does it reach the greatest height. Nevertheless it is by far the most popular geyser. Its popularity is due mainly to its regularity and dependability. You can count on Old Faithful. Nothing in life can take the place of faithfulness and dependability. It is one of the greatest virtues. Brilliance, genius, competence—all are subservient to the quality of faithfulness."

Are you a faithful person? If your family and friends were asked that question about you, what would they say? If there is room for improvement, you can count on God to help you. He is the Faithful One.

LET YOUR ACTIONS
BACK UP YOUR WORDS

When Teddy Roosevelt was asked to give a speech to the Naval War College in Newport, Rhode Island, on June 2, 1897, his theme was "Readiness." He insisted the only way to keep peace was to be ready for war, and the only way to be ready for war was to enlarge the navy. It was a rousing, patriotic speech. The following February, the Maine was blown up, killing 264 sailors, and Americans across the land cried, "Remember the Maine!" In April, President McKinley asked Congress to declare war.

For obvious reasons, Americans were not surprised that Roosevelt backed the war effort. Most Americans were surprised, however, when Teddy Roosevelt resigned from his position as assistant secretary of the navy three weeks after the war declaration so that he'd be ready to fight. His friends told him he was crazy for throwing away his political future. His wife was against it. Yet all who knew Roosevelt well knew, even as they made them, that their protests were in vain. He had to join the effort. He later wrote that he wanted to be able to tell his children why he had fought in the war, not why he hadn't fought in it. As far as he was concerned, a person simply couldn't preach one thing and then do another.

That kind of attitude is what will separate you from the pack and cause you to be a great man or woman in life. When your actions line up with your words, a tremendous reputation will follow.

MEN ARE ALIKE IN THEIR PROMISES. IT IS ONLY IN THEIR DEEDS THAT THEY DIFFER.

MOLIERE

Many a man claims to have unfailing love, but a faithful man who can find?

PROVERBS 20:6 NIV

The wise in HEART
accept commands,
but a chattering fool
comes to ruin.

PROVERBS 10:8 NIV

READY OBEDIENCE

THE STORY IS TOLD OF A great military captain who, after a full day of battle, sat by a warming fire with several of his officers and began talking over the events of the day.

He asked them, "Who did the best today on the field of battle?"

One officer told of a man who had fought bravely all day and then just before dusk had been severely wounded. Another told of a man who had taken a hit for a fellow soldier, sparing his friend's life but possibly losing his own. Yet another told of the man who had led the charge into battle. Still another told of a solider who had risked his life to pull a fellow soldier into a trench.

The captain heard them out and then said, "No, I fear you are all mistaken. The best man in the field today was the soldier who was just lifting up his arm to strike the enemy, but, upon hearing the trumpet sound the retreat, checked himself, dropped his arm without striking the blow, and retreated. That perfect and ready obedience to the will of his general is the noblest thing that was done today on the battlefield."

That's the kind of obedience God desires from us—immediate and complete.

Who's Who:

Jonah

The story of Jonah has been called the biggest fish story of all time. Jonah was a prophet of God. His job was to go where God sent him and say what God told him to say.

Well . . . Jonah did a pretty good job of being a prophet until God sent him to the city of Nineveh. You know the story—instead of obeying God and calling the citizens of the city to turn from their sinful behavior and back to God, Jonah ran away and ended up in the belly of a huge fish. That's where he stayed for three days and three nights.

By the time the fish vomited up Jonah on dry land, he had learned his lesson and was ready to do as God had asked him.

Why did Jonah disobey God? Surprisingly, it was because he knew that if he convinced the sinful people of Nineveh to repent, God would forgive them. That ticked him off. Jonah yelled at God, "I knew it—when I was back home, I knew this was going to happen! That's why I ran off to Tarshish! I knew you were sheer grace and mercy, not easily angered, rich in love, and ready at the drop of a hat to turn your plans of punishment into a program of forgiveness!" (Jonah 4:2 MSG)

PIERCE THE DARKNESS

Have you ever watched an icicle form? Did you notice how the dripping water froze, one drop at a time, until the icicle was a foot long or more?

If the water was clean, the icicle remained clear and sparkled brightly in the sun; but if the water was slightly muddy, the icicle looked cloudy, its beauty spoiled.

Our character is formed in the same way. Each thought or feeling adds its layer of influence. Each decision we make—about matters both great and small—contributes. Every outside influence that we take into our minds and souls—be they impressions, experiences, visual images, or the words of others—helps build our character.

> CHARACTER IS WHAT YOU ARE IN THE DARK.
>
> DWIGHT L. MOODY

We must remain concerned at all times about the droplets that we allow to drip into our lives. Just as habits born of hate, falsehood, and evil intent mar and eventually destroy us, acts that develop habits of love, truth, and goodness silently mold and fashion us into the image of God.

When you build a clear, sparkling character, the light reflected through you will pierce the darkness around you.

THE INTEGRITY OF THE UPRIGHT WILL GUIDE THEM.
PROVERBS 11:3 NASB

WISE WORDS

What lies before us
and what lies behind
us are small matters
compared to what lies
within us. And when
we bring what is within
out into the world,
miracles happen.

HENRY DAVID THOREAU

HOW Do YOU MEASURE Up?

When you take an honest look at yourself, do you see a person:

1. Who is limited.
2. Who has unlimited potential.
3. Whom you don't know.

What do you feel are your greatest strengths and God-given gifts, those qualities that comprise your unique potential? On a separate piece of paper, make a list of your natural, spontaneous talents—those things you enjoy the most—and where those gifts point you. Then ask God to broaden your inner image so you can contain all that He has created you to be.

BREAK FREE FROM LIMITATIONS

> **ADVERSITY**
> CAUSES SOME MEN
> TO BREAK; OTHERS
> TO BREAK
> RECORDS.
> WILLIAM A. WARD

As a senior in high school, Jim averaged a .427 at bat and led his team in home runs. He also quarterbacked his football team to the state semifinals. Jim later went on to pitch professionally for the New York Yankees.

That's a remarkable achievement for any athlete; but it's an almost unbelievable one for Jim, who was born without a right hand.

A little boy who had only parts of two fingers on one of his hands once came to Jim in the clubhouse after a Yankees' game and said, "They call me 'Crab' at camp. Did kids ever tease you?"

"Yeah," Jim replied. "Kids used to tell me that my hand looked like a foot." Then he asked the boy an all-important question, "Is there anything you can't do?" The boy answered, "No."

"Well, I don't think so either," Jim responded.

Today, what others see as a limitation is only a limitation if you think it is. God certainly doesn't see you as limited—He sees you as having unlimited potential. When we begin to see ourselves the way God sees us, there are no records that we can't break!

If you faint in the day of adversity, your strength is small.

PROVERBS 24:10 NKJV

LEAVE A LASTING IMPRESSION

When Salvation Army Officer Shaw saw the three men before him, tears sprang to his eyes. Shaw was a medical missionary who had just arrived in India. He had been assigned to a leper colony that the Salvation Army was taking over. The three men before him had manacles and fetters binding their hands and feet. Their bonds were painfully cutting into their diseased flesh. Captain Shaw turned to the guard and said, "Please unfasten the chains."

> **The only** letter I need is you yourselves! . . . They can see that you are a letter from Christ, written by us . . . not one carved on stone, but in human hearts.
>
> 2 CORINTHIANS 3:2-3 TLB

"It isn't safe," the guard protested. "These men are dangerous criminals as well as lepers!"

"I'll be responsible," Captain Shaw said. "They are suffering enough." He then reached out, took the keys, knelt, tenderly removed the shackles from the men, and treated their bleeding ankles and wrists.

About two weeks later, Shaw had to make an overnight trip. He dreaded leaving his wife and child alone. The words of the guard came back to him, and he was concerned about the safety of his family. When Shaw's wife went to the front door the morning she was alone, she was startled to see the three criminals lying on her steps. One of them explained, "We know the doctor go. We stay here all night so no harm come to you."

Even dangerous men are capable of responding to an act of love! Touched lives are the most important monuments you can leave. When you treat people with that kind of love, you are impressing your name upon their hearts.

Carve your name on hearts and not on marble.

CHARLES H. SPURGEON

JUST DO IT

to do | urgent

#1 **Carve your name upon a few hearts this week. Make a list and identify five people who are ill or need special encouragement. This could be a friend, a teacher, an elderly person from your church, a single parent, or someone who has just lost a loved one. The possibilities are endless.**

#2

Write an encouraging personal note on one side of an index card. On the other side include a scripture with the person's name written in the space like this:

#3 I always give thanks to God for you, _____, and mention you in my prayers, constantly remembering before our God and Father your work of faith and labor of love and steadfastness of hope in our Lord Jesus Christ (1 Thessalonians 1:2 NRSV).

#4 Sign your name and remember to pray for each one.

#5

#6

#7

#8

booklist

read more about it...
integrity

- *Way to Life: Christian Practices for Teens*
  by Dorothy C. Bass, Don C. Richter

- *Stop Pretending*
  by Luis Palau

- *YouthWalk*
  by Bruce H. Wilkinson

- *Honey for a Teen's Heart*
  by Gladys M. Hunt, Barbara Hampton

- *Checklist for Life for Teens: Timeless
  Wisdom and Foolproof Strategies for
  Making the Most of Life's Challenges and
  Opportunities*

- *Beyond Integrity*
  by Scott B. Rae, Kenman L. Wong

BE CAREFUL
WHAT YOU PROMISE

A MAN WHO had been quite successful in the manufacturing business decided to retire. He called in his son to tell him of his decision, saying, "Son, it's all yours as of the first of next month." The son, while eager to take over the firm and exert his own brand of leadership, also realized what a big responsibility he was facing. "I'd be grateful for any words of advice you have to give me," he said to his father.

The father advised, "Well, I've made a success of this business because of two principles: reliability and wisdom. First, take reliability. If you promise goods by the tenth of the month, no matter what happens, you must deliver by the tenth. Your customers won't understand any delay. They'll see a delay as failure. So even if it costs you overtime, double time, or golden time, you must deliver on your promise."

The son mulled this over for a few moments and then asked, "And wisdom?" The father shot back: "Wisdom is never making such a stupid promise in the first place."

Carefully weigh your ability to back up your words with evidence, and be sure you can deliver on a promise before you make it. A large part of your reputation is your ability to keep your word.

> **One-half** the trouble of this life can be traced to saying "yes" too quick, and not saying "no" soon enough.
> BENJAMIN FRANKLIN

Do you see a man who is hasty in his words? There is more hope for a fool than for him.

PROVERBS 29:20 NASB

THE RIGHT PLACE
AT THE RIGHT TIME

YOU CAN AC-COMPLISH MORE IN ONE HOUR WITH GOD THAN ONE LIFETIME WITHOUT HIM.

THE LORD appeared to a man named Ananias in a vision and asked him to undertake what Ananias must surely have perceived as a dangerous mission. He directed him to go to the house of a man named Judas, lay his hands on a man named Saul of Tarsus, and pray that he might receive his sight. Saul had been blinded while traveling to Damascus to persecute the Christians there, having the full intent of taking them captive to Jerusalem for trial, torture, and death. Even so, Ananias did as the Lord asked him, and within the hour, Saul's sight was restored.

According to Christian legend, Ananias was a simple cobbler who had no idea what happened to Saul after that day, or how he had changed the course of human history by obeying God in a simple act that was part of Saul's transformation into the apostle Paul. As he lay on his deathbed, Ananias looked up toward Heaven and whispered, "I haven't done much, Lord: a few shoes sewn, a few sandals stitched. But what more could be expected of a poor cobbler?"

The Lord spoke in Ananias' heart, "Don't worry, Ananias, about how much you have accomplished—or how little. You were there in the hour I needed you, and that is all that matters."

Being in the right place at the right time, even if it's only for one hour, can give you the opportunity to change history. In order to be there, you must simply listen and obey.

"With God all things are possible."

MATTHEW 19:26 NIV

TOP 10 TIPS for Being in the Right Place at the Right Time for God to Use You.

1. ASK GOD TO PLACE YOU AT THE CENTER OF HIS WILL.

2. ASK TO BE USED OF GOD ON A DAILY BASIS.

3. GO ABOUT YOUR DAILY ROUTINE EXPECTING GOD TO FULFILL HIS DESTINY FOR YOU.

4. BE READY AND AWARE WHEN GOD OFFERS OPPORTUNITIES.

5. DON'T MINIMIZE THE SMALL THINGS IN LIFE.

6. PRAY EACH MORNING FOR GOD TO OPEN DOORS TO USE YOU THAT DAY.

7. TRUST THAT YOU ARE IN GOD'S WILL EVEN WHEN THE EVIDENCE IS NOT APPARENT.

8. GO WHERE YOU SEE GOD'S WORK BEING DONE.

9. KEEP A POSITIVE ATTITUDE.

10. BELIEVE THAT GOD WILL COMPLETE THE GOOD WORK THAT HE HAS BEGUN IN YOU.

CONSIDER
THIS!

Fear imprisons,
    Faith liberates;
Fear paralyzes,
    Faith empowers;
Fear disheartens,
    Faith encourages;
Fear sickens,
    Faith heals;
Fear makes useless,
    Faith makes serviceable;
Fear puts hopelessness at the heart of God,
    Faith rejoices in its God.
—H.E. Fosdick

STAND FIRM
IN YOUR FAITH

Former President Harry S Truman once remarked that no president of our nation has ever escaped abuse and even libel from the press. He noted that it was far more common than rare to find a president publicly called a traitor. Truman further concluded that the president who had not fought with Congress or the Supreme Court hadn't done his job.

What is true for an American president is also true for everyone else. No matter how small a person's job may be—no matter how low he may be on a particular organizational chart or strata of society—there will be those who oppose him, ridicule him, and perhaps even challenge him to a fight. That is why no person can

IF YOU DON'T STAND FOR SOMETHING, YOU'LL FALL FOR ANYTHING!

expect to conduct himself as if he were trying to win a popularity contest. Rather, a person needs to chart the course he feels compelled to walk in life and then do so with head held high and his convictions intact. It's simply a matter of taking life in stride to recognize that every person will eventually face the test of ridicule and criticism as he upholds his principles or defends his morals.

It's inevitable that you will be criticized or attacked sometime in your life, but collapsing from fear of an attack isn't inevitable. Stand firm in your faith, and the Lord will stand with you!

"If you do not stand firm in your faith,
you will not stand at all."

Isaiah 7:9 niv

KEEP YOUR PROMISES

The former president of Baylor University, Rufus C. Burleson, once told an audience, "How often I have heard my father paint in glowing words the honesty of his old friend Colonel Ben Sherrod. When he was threatened with bankruptcy and destitution in old age and was staggering under a debt of $850,000, a contemptible lawyer told him, 'Colonel Sherrod, you are hopelessly ruined, but if you will furnish me $5,000 as a witness fee, I can pick a technical flaw in the whole thing and get you out of it.'"

"The grand old Alabamian said, 'Your proposition is insulting. I signed the notes in good faith, and the last dollar shall be paid if charity digs my grave and buys my shroud.' [My father] carried me and my brother Richard once especially to see that incorruptible old man, and his face and words are imprinted upon my heart and brain."

People will remember us for our kept promises and our honesty, especially when we could have profited from not telling the truth. The character of your word is your greatest asset, and honesty is your best virtue.

> **LEARN TO SAY "NO"; IT WILL BE OF MORE USE TO YOU THAN TO BE ABLE TO READ LATIN.**
>
> CHARLES H. SPURGEON

JUST SAY A SIMPLE YES OR NO, SO THAT YOU WILL NOT SIN.

JAMES 5:12 TLB

WISE WORDS

One of the simplest and most effective ways I know to educate or strengthen our accountability is to make and keep promises; to learn what we are capable of doing with our unique potential, and what others are capable of doing with theirs, and then openly saying what we will commit to and committing to what we say. . . . Integrity is not a personality trait, it's a character trait. It is strong and purposeful. It is deep and reflective.

ROBERT COOPER, AYMAN SAWAF

Facts

It is said that about 200 years ago, the tomb of the great conqueror, Charlemagne, was opened. The sight the workmen saw was startling. There was his body in a sitting position, clothed in the most elaborate of kingly garments, with a scepter in his bony hand. On his knee there lay a New Testament, with a cold lifeless finger pointing to Mark 8:36: "For what shall it profit a man, if he shall gain the whole world, and lose his own soul?"

This particular emperor knew what his values were and expressed them even in death. Can you identify your values? Take out a sheet of paper and write them down. Tack them on your bedroom wall or post them on the refrigerator so that your actions each day line up with your values.

SOLID VALUES FOR A SOLID FOUNDATION

It's not hard to make decisions when you know what your values are.

Roy Disney

Marshall Field once offered the following twelve reminders to help a person obtain a sound sense of values:

1. The value of time.
2. The success of perseverance.
3. The pleasure of working.
4. The dignity of simplicity.
5. The worth of character.
6. The power of kindness.
7. The influence of example.
8. The obligation of duty.
9. The wisdom of economy.
10. The virtue of patience.
11. The improvement of talent.
12. The joy of originating.

Can you state the core principles of your value system today? For some, it is likely to be the Ten Commandments. For others, it is the sayings of Jesus.

Solid values are like unblemished, evenly-hewn stones. No matter what you build with them, you can be sure that if you follow the basic laws of construction, the structure will be solid, and all your decisions will stand firm.

Daniel resolved not to defile himself.

DANIEL 1:8 NIV

PLANT SEEDS FROM GOD'S BOOK

A BIBLE–CAREFULLY READ and well worn–was the most important book in Gerrit's house. His home was a house of prayer, where many tears were shed in intercession for revival in his church in Heemstede. Almost a generation later, his prayers were answered as that very church became the center of an upsurge of faith in Holland—part of the Great Awakening in Europe.

When she was about eighteen years old, Gerrit's great-granddaughter had a dream about him. He was walking through a beautiful park with her, and he said, "When you sow some seed and put it in the ground, this seed will make a plant, and this plant will give seed again. . . . You, my dear Corrie, are the daughter of my grandson. . . . You are a plant, blooming from my seed. I will show you something that will never be changed. It is the Word of God." In the dream, he opened his Bible and said, "This book will be the same forever." He then told her, "Plant the seeds from God's Book, and they will grow from generation to generation."

Corrie ten Boom did just that. She planted God's Word in hearts and minds around the world. Information learned in textbooks is continually updated, and courses of study change; but the truths of the Bible are absolutes. Its promises are sure. Plant its seeds in your heart.

lighten up

Preparing for a long trip, the young Christian said to his friend, "I am just about packed. I only have to put in a guidebook, a lamp, a mirror, a microscope, a telescope, a volume of fine poetry, a few biographies, a package of old letters, a book of songs, a sword, a hammer, and a set of books I have been studying."

"But," the friend objected, "you can't get all that into your bag."

"Oh, yes," replied the young man, "it doesn't take much room." He placed his Bible in the corner of the suitcase and closed the lid.

All Scripture is inspired by God and is useful to what is wrong in our lives.

"A knowledge of the Bible without a college course is more valuable than a college course without the Bible."

WILLIAM LYON PHELPS

teach us what is true and to make us realize
2 TIMOTHY 3:16-17 NLT

I can do all things
through Him
who strengthens me.

PHILIPPIANS 4:13 NASB

> **Clear your mind of can't.**
>
> SAMUEL JOHNSON

I CAN!

HARRY HOUDINI, WHO won fame as an escape artist early in the twentieth century, issued a challenge wherever he went. He claimed he could be locked in any jail cell in the country and set himself free within minutes. He had done it over and over in every city he visited.

One time, however, something seemed to go wrong. Houdini entered a jail cell in his street clothes. The heavy metal doors clanged shut behind him, and he took from his belt a concealed piece of strong but flexible metal. He set to work on the lock to his cell, but something seemed different about this particular lock. He worked for thirty minutes, but nothing happened. An hour passed. This was long after the time that Houdini normally freed himself, and he began to sweat and pant in exasperation. Still, he could not pick the lock.

Finally, after laboring for two hours, frustrated and feeling a sense of failure closing in around him, Houdini leaned against the door he could not unlock. To his amazement, it swung open! It had never been locked!

How many times are challenges impossible—or doors locked—only because we think they are? When we focus our minds and energy toward them and strike the word "can't" from our vocabulary, those impossible tasks turn into attainable goals.

Who's Who:

Joni Eareckson

Every door seems to slam shut for young Joni Eareckson one July day in 1967. Diving in the murky waters of Chesapeake Bay, she suddenly felt her head strike something hard and her body spin out of control.

In those first terrible months after the accident, Joni felt that her life was over. Paralyzed from the chest down, she felt she had nothing to look forward to but suffering. God had other plans.

Joni Eareckson Tada is now a wife, a painter, an author, and a public speaker in great demand. She has inspired people around the world with her "can do" attitude and complete trust in her precious heavenly Father. More than thirty years after her accident, she has tackled the impossible countless times, and with God's help, emerged a winner!

CHOOSE THE RIGHT TEAM

In his book *The Mind of Watergate,* psychiatrist Leo Rangell, M.D., relates what he calls a "compromise of integrity" as he analyzes the relationship between former President Richard M. Nixon and several of his closest confidants. He records a conversation between investigative committee member Senator Howard Baker and young Herbert L. Porter.

Baker: "Did you ever have any qualms about what you were doing? Did you ever think of saying, 'I do not think this is quite right.' Did you ever think of that?"

Porter: "Yes, I did."

Baker: "What did you do about it?"

Porter: "I did not do anything."

Baker: "Why didn't you?"

Porter: "In all honesty, probably because of the fear of the group pressure that would ensue, of not being a team player."

> **The rotten** apple spoils his companion.
>
> BENJAMIN FRANKLIN

There's nothing wrong with being a team player as long as you choose the right team! You will become like your friends, even as they change and become a little more like you. Therefore, choose your friends cautiously and thoughtfully.

He who walks with wise men will be wise, but the companion of fools will be destroyed.

PROVERBS 13:20 NKJV

My friends get upset with me when I won't party with them, but I don't want to drink and smoke, and that's the main thing they do when they party. What should I do?

First of all, I wonder if you're making the best choices in friends. Sometimes we make friends without thinking about it much. Whomever we gravitate toward, or whoever gravitates toward us, we make our friend. But who we spend time with will influence us for good or for bad. Try being more proactive in choosing friends. For instance, sit down and make a list of the qualities you seek to develop in your own life. Then make a list of your friends and check their character against your list of desired qualities. How do they measure up?

God expects us as Christians to follow the example that Christ left us. In other words, He wants us to mirror the way Christ lived. That is not always easy, but it can be almost impossible if we are influenced by unbelieving friends. Go ahead and tell your friends why you don't want to party with them. They may not show it at first, but deep inside they will respect you for having the courage to stand by your convictions. Don't give up on them completely, your example may someday lead them to accept Christ, but try to add a few Christian friends who share your beliefs and lifestyle. Chances are, they will support you in your Christian walk and not ask you to do things that offend your faith.

HOW Do YOU MEASURE Up?

Answer Yes or No to the following statements.

I am able to speak out when:
1. Someone uses the Lord's name in vain.
2. I see a person bullying another.
3. I observe an injustice.
4. A friend needs defending.
5. A friend needs accountability.
6. I have wronged someone.

Give some thought to your answers. Are there any answers you would like to change?

THE COURAGE
TO SPEAK OUT

I WOULD RATHER FAIL IN THE CAUSE THAT SOME-DAY WILL TRIUMPH THAN TRIUMPH IN A CAUSE THAT SOME-DAY WILL FAIL.

WOODROW WILSON

When Honorious was emperor of Rome, the great Coliseum was often filled to overflowing with spectators who came from near and far to watch the state-sponsored games. Part of the sport consisted of human beings doing battle with wild beasts or one another—to the death. The assembled multitudes made holiday of such sport and found the greatest delight when a human being died.

One such day, a Syrian monk named Telemachus was part of the vast crowd in the arena. Telemachus was cut to the core by the utter disregard he saw for the value of human life. He leaped from the spectator stands into the arena during a gladiatorial show and cried out, "This thing is not right! This thing must stop!"

Because he had interfered, the authorities commanded that Telemachus be run through with a sword, which was done. He died, but not in vain. His cry kindled a small flame in the nearly burned-out conscience of the people, and within a matter of months, the gladiatorial combats came to an end.

The greater the wrong, the louder we must cry out against it. The finer the cause, the louder we must applaud.

Now thanks be to God who always leads us in triumph in Christ.

2 CORINTHIANS 2:14 NKJV

BEING A LEADER

In 1643, a young shoemaker's apprentice went to Leicestershire, England, for a business fair. While there, a cousin invited him to share a jug of beer with him and another friend in the pub where they had gone to eat. Being thirsty, he joined them.

After each of the men had drunk a glass apiece, the man's cousin and friend began to drink to the health of first this one and then the other. They agreed that the person who didn't join in with their toasts would have to pay for the jug. This shocked the serious shoemaker's apprentice. He rose from the table, took out a coin, and said simply, "If it be so, I will leave you."

At that, he left the pub and spent much of the night walking up and down the streets of the city, praying and crying to the Lord. The Lord spoke to him these words as recorded in his journal: "Thou seest how young people go together into vanity and old people into the earth. Thou must forsake all—young and old—keep out of all, and be as a stranger unto all." In obedience to this command, the young man left his relations and his home and became a wanderer in England. His name? George Fox, the founder of the Quakers.

If you want to be a leader in life, you will reach a day when you will have to turn your back on people who want to waste their lives. Turn toward those who will lead you, and most of all to the One who will lead you—your Father God.

A MAN WHO WANTS TO LEAD THE ORCHESTRA MUST TURN HIS BACK ON THE CROWD.

"SO LEAVE THE CORRUPTION AND COMPROMISE; LEAVE IT FOR GOOD," SAYS GOD. "DON'T LINK UP WITH THOSE WHO WILL POLLUTE YOU. I WANT YOU ALL FOR MYSELF."

2 CORINTHIANS 6:17 MSG

WiSe WoRdS

In order to be a leader a person must have followers. And to have followers, a person must have their confidence. Hence the supreme quality for a leader is unquestionably integrity. Without it, no real success is possible, no matter whether it is on a section gang, a football field, in an army, or in an office. If a person's associates find him or her guilty of phoniness, if they find that he or she lacks forthright integrity, that person will fail. A leader's teachings and actions must square with each other. The first great need, therefore, is integrity and high purpose.

DWIGHT EISENHOWER

CONSIDER
THIS!

How Do you Spell Fearless?

Follow Christ with your whole heart.

Engage in relationships.

Approach life with passion.

Revel in joy.

Let others know how you feel.

Express your ideas.

Stand firmly in your faith.

Share your dreams.

TAKE THE RISK AND EXPERIENCE LIFE

Two baseball coaches were commiserating about the difficulty of recruiting quality players for their teams. Said one coach, "If only I could find a man who plays every position perfectly, always gets a hit, never strikes out, and never makes a fielding error." The other coach sighed in agreement and added, "Yeah, if we could just get him to lay down his hot dog and come down out of the stands."

Playing life's game to the fullest requires taking risks. Without risk, life has little emotion, little that can be counted as exhilarating or fulfilling.

- To laugh is to risk appearing the fool.

MAN CANNOT DISCOVER NEW OCEANS UNLESS HE HAS THE COURAGE TO LOSE SIGHT OF THE SHORE.

- To weep is to risk appearing sentimental.
- To reach out for another is to risk involvement.
- To expose feelings is to risk exposing one's true self.
- To place ideas and dreams before a crowd is to risk ridicule.
- To love is to risk not being loved in return.
- To live is to risk dying.
- To hope is to risk despair.
- To try is to risk failure.

Yet the person who risks nothing does nothing, has nothing, and ultimately becomes nothing. Don't be afraid to go for it. Get down out of the stands and play ball!

Peter got out of the boat, and walked on the water and came toward Jesus.

MATTHEW 14:29 NASB

RESOLVE TO SUCCEED

> ALWAYS BEAR IN MIND THAT YOUR OWN RESOLUTION TO SUCCESS IS MORE IMPORTANT THAN ANY OTHER ONE THING.
>
> ABRAHAM LINCOLN

FAMOUS STAGE and film actress Helen Hayes believed her resoluteness about her own potential for success played an important role at the beginning of her career. She once told the story of a particular audition: "Before the authors gave me the script, they observed, in a matter-of-course manner, 'Of course you play piano? You'll have to sing to your own accompaniment in the piece.' As these alarming tidings were in the course of being made, I caught a bewildered look in my mother's eyes, and so I spoke up before she could. 'Certainly I play piano,' I answered.

"As we left the theater, my mother sighed, 'I hate to see you start under a handicap,' she said. 'What made you say you could play piano?' 'The feeling that I will play before rehearsals begin,' I said. We went at once to try to rent a piano and ended by buying one. I began lessons at once, practiced finger exercises till I could no longer see the notes—and began rehearsals with the ability to accompany myself. Since then, I have never lived too far from a piano."

What you believe about your own potential for success counts far more than what any other person may believe. Believe what God believes about you—you were created for success.

The Lord GOD will help me;
Therefore I will not be disgraced;
Therefore I have set my face like a flint,
and I know that I will not be ashamed.

ISAIAH 50:7 NKJV

TOP 10 TIPS

for Believing in Yourself

1. OBJECTIVELY EVALUATE YOUR GOD-GIVEN GIFTS.

2. WRITE DOWN YOUR GIFTS AND POST THEM ON THE WALL IN YOUR BEDROOM.

3. CHANGE THE NEGATIVE MENTAL MESSAGES YOU TELL YOURSELF TO POSITIVE STATEMENTS.

4. LOOK FOR YOUR POSSIBILITIES, NOT YOUR LIMITATIONS.

5. WORK DELIBERATELY TO PRACTICE YOUR SKILLS AND GROW THEM.

6. NEVER GIVE UP.

7. REMEMBER THAT MISTAKES ARE FERTILE GROUND FOR GROWTH AND SUCCESS.

8. BELIEVE THAT WITH HARD WORK YOU CAN ACCOMPLISH ANYTHING.

9. KNOW THAT GOD HAS A PURPOSE FOR YOUR LIFE.

10. MEMORIZE AND QUOTE SCRIPTURES THAT REMIND YOU OF GOD'S FAITHFULNESS.

booklist

read more about it...
overcoming difficulties

- *Be Patient: God Isn't Finished with Me Yet (Teen Edition)*

- *Dealing with the Stuff that Makes Life Tough: The 10 Things That Stress Teen Girls Out and How to Cope with Them*
  by Jill Zimmerman Rutledge

- *Failing Forward: How to Make the Most of Your Mistakes*
  by John C. Maxwell

- *God's Little Instruction Book for Teens: Getting an Edge on Life*

- *It's a Jungle in Here: Devotions for Teens*
  by Dale Larsen, editor

- *Stand Your Ground: Devotions for Teens*

- *Wrestling with God: Prayer That Never Gives Up*
  by Greg Laurie

RISING TO THE CHALLENGE

WHEN AARON WAS months old, he stopped gaining weight. A few months later, his hair began to fall out. At first, doctors told Aaron's parents that he would be short as an adult but otherwise normal. Later, a pediatrician diagnosed the problem as progeria, or rapid aging. Just as the pediatrician predicted, Aaron never grew beyond three feet in height, had no hair on his head or body, looked like an old man while still a child, and died of old age in his early teens. His father, a rabbi, felt a deep, aching sense of unfairness.

About a year and a half after Aaron's death, the father came to realize that none of us is ever promised a life free of pain or disappointment. Rather, the most any of us has been promised is that we need not be alone in our pain and that we can draw upon a source outside ourselves for strength and courage. He came to the conclusion that God does not cause our misfortunes but rather helps us by inspiring others to help.

> **Little Minds** are tamed and subdued by misfortune; but great minds rise above them.
> WASHINGTON IRVING

Out of Harold Kushner's experience came a book that has helped millions, *When Bad Things Happen to Good People.* He says, "I think of Aaron and all that his life taught me, and I realize how much I have lost and how much I have gained. Yesterday seems less painful, and I am not afraid of tomorrow."

When you stop looking at the difficulties in your life as obstacles and start seeing them as stepping stones, you will begin to rise above your difficulties and gain something from them. They will make you stronger and wiser.

A righteous man falls seven times and rises again.

PROVERBS 24:16 AMP

LISTEN UP

An American Indian was once visiting New York City; and as he walked the busy Manhattan streets with a friend from the city, he suddenly stopped, tilted his head to one side, and said, "I hear a cricket."

"You're crazy," his friend said. The Cherokee answered, "No, I hear a cricket. I do! I'm sure of it."

The friend replied, "It's the noon hour. People are jammed on the sidewalks, cars are honking, taxis are whizzing by, the city is full of noise. And you think you can hear a cricket?"

If you listen to constructive criticism, you will be at home among the wise.

PROVERBS 15:31 NLT

"I'm sure I do," said the visitor. He listened even more closely and then walked to the corner, spotted a shrub in a large cement planter, dug into the leaves underneath it, and pulled out a cricket. His friend was astounded. The man said, "The fact is, my friend, that my ears are different than yours. It all depends on what your ears have been tuned to hear. Let me show you." At that, he reached into his pocket, pulled out a handful of loose change, and dropped the coins on the pavement. Every head within a half block turned. "See what I mean?" he said, picking up the coins. "It all depends on what you are listening for."

Listen today to those things that will make you wise. Don't neglect those things that will prepare you for eternity.

A good listener is not only popular everywhere, but after a while he knows something.

WILSON MIZNER

☑ JUST DO IT

#1 **It's hard to miss the fact that God gave each of us two ears and one mouth. Could that be because our lives just work better when we listen twice as much as we talk? Improve your listening skills by trying these helpful suggestions:**

#2
- Make eye contact.
- Don't let distractions interrupt your attention.

#3
- Include body language, rise and fall in tonal inflections, and countenance in your observations to understand fully what is being expressed.

#4
- Smile and nod your head to affirm your interest and attentiveness.

- Pay attention to what the person is saying instead of concentrating on your response.

#5
- Mirror back what has just been said. For instance, "So what I'm hearing is that you feel. . . ."

#6

#7

#8

#9

#10

KEEP GOING

AMERICAN SPORTS FANS watched in awe on Sunday, March 4, 1979, as Phil took to the giant-slalom slopes at Whiteface Mountain, New York. He exploded onto the course and then settled into a powerful carving of the mountainside. Nonetheless, at gate thirty-five, tragedy struck. Phil hooked his inside ski on a pole, went flying head over heels, and crashed in a crumpled heap. The ski team physician described the injury as "the ultimate broken ankle"— a break of both the ankle and lower leg. He had to put the bones back together with a three-inch metal plate and seven screws.

The question was not whether Phil would ever ski again but if he would ever walk again. Looking back, Phil describes the months after his injury as a time of deep despair. Still, he never entertained doubts about walking or skiing.

After two months on crutches and a high-discipline exercise program, he forced himself to walk without limping. In August, he began skiing gentle slopes. Less than six months after the accident, he entered a race in Australia and finished second. In February of 1980, less than a year after his agonizing injury, Phil Mahre took on the same mountain where he had fallen, and he won an Olympic silver medal.

When defeat and despair threaten to overtake you and squash your dreams, keep on going. Eventually, you will overtake defeat with victory and despair with joy!

lighten up

If you're ever tempted to give up, just think of Brahms who took seven long years to compose his famous lullaby. He kept falling asleep at the piano.

—Robert Orben

A great oak is only a little nut that held his ground.

—L&N Magazine

Consider the postage stamp: Its usefulness consists in the ability to stick to one thing till it gets there.

—Josh Billings

" Never despair; but if you do, work on in despair. **"**

TERENCE

your work will be rewarded. 2 CHRONICLES 15:7 NIV

Fun Facts

Purnell Bailey offers this interesting information: "The Bureau of Standards in Washington . . . tells us that a dense fog covering seven city blocks, 100 feet deep, is composed of something less than one glass of water. That amount of water is divided into some 60 thousand million tiny drops. Not much there! Yet when those minute particles settle down over the city or countryside they can blot out practically all vision.

"A cupful of worry does just about the same thing. We forget to trust God. The tiny drops of fretfulness close around our thoughts and we are submerged without vision."

STAYING COOL

Don't cross your **bridges** until you get to them.
We **spend our lives** defeating ourselves crossing
bridges we **never get to**.

BOB BALES

During the four-week siege of Tientsin, during the Boxer Rebellion of June 1900, Herbert Hoover helped erect barricades around the foreign compound and organized all the able-bodied men into a protective force to man them. Mrs. Hoover went to work too, helping set up a hospital, taking her turn nursing the wounded, rationing food, and serving tea every afternoon to those on sentry duty. Like her husband, she remained calm and efficient throughout the crisis, and even seemed to enjoy the excitement.

One afternoon, while she sat at home playing solitaire to relax after her work at the hospital, a shell suddenly burst nearby. She ran to the back door and discovered a big hole in the backyard. A little later,

a second shell hit the road in front of the house. Then came a third shell. This one burst through one of the windows of the house and demolished a post by the staircase.

Several reporters covering the siege rushed into the living room to see if she was all right and found her calmly seated at the card table. "I don't seem to be winning this hand," she remarked coolly, "but that was the third shell and therefore the last one for the present anyway. Their pattern is three in a row." Then she suggested brightly, "Let's go and have tea."

If you think about it, you will realize most of the things you worry about never happen. Instead of worrying, relax and use your mental energy for more important things.

"Don't be anxious about tomorrow.
God will take care of your tomorrow too.
Live one day at a time."

MATTHEW 6:34 TLB

BE EXTRAORDINARY

Country-music star Randy Travis and his manager, Lib, remember the lean days of his career—all 3,650 of them. For ten years, Lib did whatever it took to keep her club open long enough for somebody to discover Travis' talent. For his part, Randy sang his heart out, and when he wasn't singing, he fried catfish or washed dishes in the kitchen. Then it happened. Everything seemed to click for him. He had a hit called "On the Other Hand," an album contract, a tour offer, and a movie deal. He was hot! Everyone seemed to be calling him an overnight success.

Travis notes, "We were turned down more than once by every label in Nashville, but I'm kind of one to believe that if you work at something long enough and keep believing, sooner or later it will happen."

In many instances in life, it's extra effort that makes the difference. Money can buy a house, but loving touches turn it into a home. A sack lunch can be a gourmet meal with a love note tucked inside. A meal is just food, but with candles and flowers, it's an occasion. Do more than is required of you today. Give the extra that makes life truly extraordinary.

THE DIFFER-ENCE BETWEEN ORDINARY AND EXTRAORDINARY IS THAT LITTLE EXTRA.

WHATEVER YOUR HAND FINDS TO DO, DO IT WITH YOUR MIGHT.

ECCLESIASTES 9:10 NKJV

WISE WORDS

The average person puts only 25 percent of his energy and ability into his work. The world takes off its hat to those who put in more than 50 percent of their capacity, and stands on its head for those few and far between souls who devote 100 percent.

ANDREW CARNEGIE

CONSIDER THIS!

A spiny caterpillar builds a cocoon around itself to morph into a beautiful butterfly. During the process of releasing itself from the chrysallis, a furious struggle ensues. The butterfly must endure this lengthy struggle in order to become strong enough to survive outside the cocoon. It has to push hard against the cocoon for a long time to strengthen its muscles enough to fly. The struggle is essential to prepare the butterfly for doing what butterflies do.

Don't view your struggles as bad things. Embrace them. Treat them like your friends. While you are going through them, keep telling yourself that they are making you strong, beefing you up, making you a better person. They will prepare you to do what God intended you to do.

HIS REWARDS
ARE BETTER THAN GOLD

These words were spelled out in lights at the 18th Olympics in Tokyo: "The most important thing in the Olympic Games is not to win but to take part; just as the most important thing in life is not the triumph but the struggle. The essential thing is ... to have fought well."

The athletes who make it to the Olympic Games are already the best of the best from each nation. Each athlete has excelled in ways few of his or her peers will ever reach. Yet only one will wear a gold medal, one a silver, and one a bronze. Those who are so accustomed to winning face the devastating possibility of losing before not only their teammates, but also their countrymen, and, in this age of worldwide television, before the entire world. How vital it is for these athletes to keep their perspective—that winning is not the important issue at the Olympics but the opportunity to compete, to try, and to give one's best effort.

Regardless of the arena in which you compete, winning is not what is truly important. Giving your best effort to a challenge is what molds within you the lasting traits and character that are better than gold.

> YOU MAY BE DISAPPOINTED IF YOU FAIL, BUT YOU ARE DOOMED IF YOU DON'T TRY.
>
> BEVERLY SILLS

The **sluggard craves** and **gets nothing,**

but the **desires** of the **diligent**

are **fully satisfied.**

PROVERBS 13:4 NIV

HOW Do YOU MEASURE Up?

How do you respond to your parents' pushing, prodding, and motivating?

A. I sit down and don't budge. I'll teach them that they can't force me to do anything.
B. I listen, then I do what I want to do.
C. I pay attention to the things they tell me to do. I realize they want what is best for me.
D. I tell them to mind their own business. Their experiences are irrelevant to me. They don't know what's up.
E. I appreciate my parents' influence on me. They've been around the block a few times and know things that I don't yet know. I can trust them to give me good advice.

Teens are prone to rebel against their parents. In fact, it is a natural response to individuation. But, parents are a major influence in motivating their children in the right direction. Maybe it's time to respond to your parents' prodding with some questions and conversation. Show them that you appreciate their concern and their wisdom.

KEEP MOVING

THE ROAD TO SUCCESS IS DOTTED WITH MANY TEMPTING PARKING PLACES.

The first thing to emerge at a baby giraffe's birth is its front hooves and head. Minutes later, the newborn is hurled from its mother's body, falls ten feet, and lands on its back. Within seconds, it rolls to an upright position with its legs tucked under its body. From this position, it views the world for the first time and shakes off any remaining birthing fluid.

The mother giraffe lowers her head just long enough to take a quick look at her calf, and then she does what seems to be a very unreasonable thing—she kicks her baby, sending it sprawling head over heels. If it doesn't get up, she kicks it again and again until the calf finally stands on its wobbly legs. Then what does the mother giraffe do? She kicks it off its feet! Why? She wants it to remember how to get up.

In the wild, baby giraffes must be able to get up as quickly as possible to stay with the herd and avoid becoming a meal for lions, hyenas, leopards, or wild hunting dogs. The best way a mother giraffe has of ensuring that her calf lives is for her to teach it to get up quickly and get with it.

Don't complain if those who love you push you into action when you'd rather be in park. They are doing you a favor.

We'd better get on with it. Strip down, start running—and never quit! No extra spiritual fat, no parasitic sins.

HEBREWS 12:1 MSG

PERSISTENCE PAYS OFF

> A GOAL PROPERLY SET IS HALFWAY REACHED.
>
> ZIG ZIGLAR

A YOUNG MAN in need of work once saw this advertisement in a Boston newspaper: "Wanted: young man as an understudy to a financial statistician, P.O. Box 1720." The young man decided this was just the kind of job he wanted, so he replied to the ad but received no answer. He wrote again and even a third time with no reply. Next, he went to the Boston post office and asked the name of the holder of Box 1720, but the clerk refused to give it, as did the postmaster.

Early one morning, an idea came to the young man. He rose early, took the first train to Boston, went to the post office, and stood watch near Box 1720. After a while, a man appeared, opened the box, and took out the mail. The young man followed him as he returned to the office of a stock brokerage firm. The young man entered and asked for the manager.

In the interview, the manager asked, "How did you find out that I was the advertiser?" The young man told about his detective work, to which the manager replied, "Young man, you are just the kind of persistent fellow I want. You are employed!"

If a goal is worthy, there's no good reason to stop pursuing it! Find something you truly want to do, then go for it with all your heart, mind, and strength.

The LORD answered me, and said: "Write the vision and make it plain on tablets, that he may run who reads it.

HABAKKUK 2:2 NKJV

TOP 10 TIPS for Persisting During a Difficult Challenge

1. KNOW WHAT YOUR GOALS ARE; REMIND YOURSELF OF THEM DAILY.

2. PRAY FOR STRENGTH AND ENDURANCE.

3. SHARE YOUR DIFFICULTIES WITH A FRIEND.

4. RECOMMIT YOURSELF TO YOUR GOALS.

5. TRY NEW IDEAS WHEN OLD ONES HAVE NOT PAID OFF THE WAY YOU WANTED.

6. BRAINSTORM NEW SOLUTIONS WITH A CREATIVE FRIEND.

7. KEEP TRYING EVEN WHEN YOU SEEM TO COME TO A DEAD END.

8. WRITE DOWN NEW STEPS TOWARD YOUR GOAL. FOLLOW UP EACH DAY.

9. KEEP YOUR PASSION ALIVE.

10. GIVE YOUR GOALS TO THE LORD; YOU'RE NOT IN THIS ALONE!

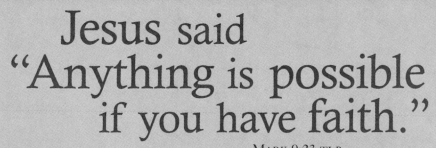

Jesus said "Anything is possible if you have faith."

MARK 9:23 TLB

> The future belongs to those who believe in the beauty of their dreams.
>
> ELEANOR ROOSEVELT

BELIEVE IN YOUR DREAM

GRACE HOPPER WAS born with a desire to discover how things worked. At age seven, her curiosity led her to dismantle every clock in her childhood home! When she grew up, she eventually completed a doctorate in mathematics at Yale University. During World War II, Grace joined the navy and was assigned to the navy's computation project at Harvard University. There she met "Harvard Mark I," the first fully functional, digital computing machine. Once again, Grace set about to learn how something worked.

Unlike the clocks in her childhood home, however, "Harvard Mark I" had 750 thousand parts and 500 miles of wire! While most experts believed computers were too complicated and expensive for anyone but highly trained scientists to use, Grace had her own idea. Her goal was to make them easier to operate so more people could use them. Her work gave rise to the programming language Cobol.

As late as 1963, each large computer had its own unique master language. Grace became an advocate for a universally accepted language. She had the audacity to envision a day when computers would one day be small enough to sit on a desk, more powerful than "Harvard Mark I," and useful in offices, schools, and at home. At the age of seventy-nine, she retired from the navy with a rank of rear admiral. More important to her, however, she had lived to see her dream of personal computers come true!

Believe in your dreams. With God, all things are possible.

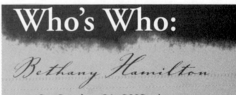

Who's Who:

Bethany Hamilton

On October 31, 2003, sixteen year old Bethany Hamilton was surfing in the crystal-clear water off Hawaii. She had been surfing since she was six years old and had no reason to think that danger was lurking nearby.

Suddenly, a shark nudged her red, white, and blue board. Before Bethany could respond, the creature took her arm off at the shoulder and then disappeared into the depths.

Bethany survived her encounter with a shark, but her dream of becoming a championship surfer seemed to be in shambles. Fortunately, Bethany wasn't ready to let her dream die. A month after her attach, she returned to the beach and would not stop until she was once again in control of her board, rushing toward the shore. In January 2004, she placed fifth in her age group in a national competition. She's determined that nothing will keep her from reaching her dreams.

FAITHFULNESS

A QUIET FOREST DWELLER who lived high above an Austrian village in the Alps was hired by a town council to keep the pristine mountain springs—the source of the town's water supply—clear of debris. With faithful regularity, the old man patrolled the hills, clearing away silt and removing leaves and branches from the springs. Over time, the village became prosperous. Mill wheels turned, farms were irrigated, and tourists came. Years passed. Then at a council meeting about the city budget, a member noticed the salary figure for the old man. He asked, "Who is he, and why do we keep him on the payroll? Has anybody seen him? For all we know, he might be dead." The council voted to dispense with his services.

For several weeks nothing changed. Then the trees began to shed their leaves. One afternoon, a town citizen noticed a brown tint to the water. Within another week, a slick covered sections of the canals, and a foul odor was detected. Sickness broke out.

The town council called a special meeting, and reversing their error in judgment, rehired the old man. Renewed life soon returned to the village as the sparkling waters returned.

Not everyone's job will make the six o'clock news every day; but no matter where God places you, do your work unto Him, and He will reward you for your faithfulness.

> **God has** no larger field for the man who is not faithfully doing his work where he is.

You have been **faithful** with a few things; I will put you in **charge** of many things.

MATTHEW 25:23 NIV

I volunteered to help at church last summer. The children's director put me in charge of cleanup at the end of each day of Vacation Bible School. I thought she would give me something more important or spiritual to do. I ended up wishing I had not volunteered. Am I wrong to feel unappreciated?

Many famous and accomplished people tell stories of their humble beginnings. As a matter of fact, this book is filled with such stories. Thumb through and find a few to remind yourself that every job has integrity. Certainly God has made it clear that He values our efforts and the intent of our hearts and will reward us for serving Him. Don't be ashamed or afraid to be humble. Humility brings its own measure of blessings. And remind yourself that God appreciates your work, no matter how humble it may seem to be.

BE STRONG AND OF GOOD COURAGE

In *The Seven Habits of Highly Effective People,* Stephen R. Covey writes: "One of the most inspiring times Sandra and I have ever had took place over a four-year period with a dear friend of ours named Carol, who had a wasting cancer disease. She had been one of Sandra's bridesmaids, and they had been best friends for over 25 years.

"When Carol was in the very last stages of the disease, Sandra spent time at her bedside helping her write her personal history. She returned from those protracted and difficult sessions almost transfixed by admiration for her friend's courage and her desire to write special messages to be given to her children at different stages in their lives.

"Carol would take as little pain-killing medication as possible, so that she had full access to her mental and emotional faculties. Then she would whisper into a tape recorder or to Sandra directly as she took notes. Carol was so proactive, so brave, and so concerned about others that she became an enormous source of inspiration to many people around her."

In today's world, perhaps one trait is needed desperately. Seek to develop it. It's called courage.

> SUCCESS IS NEVER FINAL; FAILURE IS NEVER FATAL; IT IS COURAGE THAT COUNTS.
> WINSTON CHURCHILL

BE OF GOOD COURAGE, AND HE SHALL STRENGTHEN YOUR HEART, ALL YOU WHO HOPE IN THE LORD.

PSALM 31:24 NKJV

WISE WORDS

Far better it is to dare mighty things, to win glorious triumphs, even though checkered by failure, than to take rank with those poor spirits who neither enjoy much nor suffer much, because they live in the gray twilight that knows not victory or defeat.

THEODORE ROOSEVELT

CONSIDER THIS!

Givers can be divided into three types: the flint, the sponge, and the honeycomb.

- Some givers are like a piece of flint—to get anything out of it you must hammer it, and even then you get only chips and sparks.

- Others are like a sponge—to get anything out of a sponge, you must squeeze it and squeeze it hard, because the more you squeeze a sponge, the more you get.

- But others are like a honeycomb—which just overflows with its own sweetness. That is how God gives to us, and it is how we should give to others.

BE A GIVER

A strange memorial can be found in the Mount Hope Cemetery of Hiawatha, Kansas. John M. Davis, an orphan, developed a strong dislike for his wife's family and insisted that none of his fortune go to them. He also refused requests that he eventually bequeath his estate for a hospital desperately needed in the area. Instead, after his wife died in 1930, Mr. Davis chose to invest in an elaborate tomb for himself and his wife. The tomb includes a number of statues depicting the couple at various stages of their lives. One statue is of Mr. Davis as a lonely man seated beside an empty chair. It is titled "the vacant chair." Another shows him placing a wreath in front of his wife's tombstone. Many of the statues are made of Kansas granite. No money was left for the memorial's upkeep.

> **MONEY IS LIKE AN ARM OR LEG: USE IT OR LOSE IT.**
>
> HENRY FORD

Today, largely because of its weight, this costly memorial is slowly sinking into the ground. It has become weathered and worn from the strong winds in this plains state. The townspeople regard the Davis tomb as an "old man's folly"; and many predict that within the next fifty years, the memorial will have become obliterated beyond recognition and will need to be demolished. What could have been a living legacy will eventually become granite dust.

The Bible encourages us many times not to hoard up money to be used for our own selfish desires but to be kind to the poor. When we do so, God blesses us with more. The more we give, the more we receive; and our legacy will last well into the future instead of sinking into oblivion.

Jesus said, "To him who has will more be given . . . and he will have great plenty; but from him who has not, even the little he has will be taken away."

MATTHEW 13:12 TLB

CONSIDER THIS!

Some of the most enduring literary names have received scathing reviews of their timeless classics. Below are a few taken from "Rotten Reviews," edited by Bill Henderson.

• **On "Alice in Wonderland," Lewis Carroll, 1865**

Review: "We fancy that any real child might be more puzzled than enchanted by this stiff, overwrought story."

• **On Emily Dickinson**

Review: "An eccentric, dreamy, half-educated recluse in an out-of-the-way New England village . . . Oblivion lingers in the immediate neighborhood."

• **On Charles Dickens**

Review: "We do not believe in the permanence of his reputation . . . our children will wonder what their ancestors could have meant by putting Mr. Dickens at the head of the novelists of his day."

• **On "Moby Dick," Herman Melville, 1851**

Review: "A huge dose of hyperbolical slang, maudlin sentimentalism and tragic-comic bubble and squeak."

• **On "The Adventures of Huckleberry Finn," Mark Twain, 1884**

Review: "A gross trifling with every fine feeling . . . Mr. Clemens has no reliable sense of propriety."

NEVER QUIT

In 1894, a sixteen-year-old found this note from his rhetorical teacher at Harrow, in England, attached to his report card: "A conspicuous lack of success." The young man kept on trying and went on to become one of the most famous speakers of the twentieth century. His name was Winston Churchill.

In 1902, an aspiring twenty-eight-year-old writer received a rejection letter from the poetry editor of the *Atlantic Monthly*. Returned, with a batch of poems he had sent, was this curt note: "Our magazine has no room for your vigorous verse." He kept on trying, however, and went on to see his work published. The poet's name was Robert Frost.

In 1905, the University of Bern turned down a Ph.D. dissertation as being fanciful and irrelevant. The young physics student who wrote the dissertation kept on trying and went on to develop some of his ideas into widely accepted theories. His name was Albert Einstein.

When rejection shakes your resolve and dims your goals, keep on trying. If you do not quit, one day you will be living out your dreams!

IN TRYING TIMES, DON'T QUIT TRYING.

The righteous will move onward and forward, and those with pure hearts will become stronger and stronger.

JOB 17:9 NLT

fyi booklist

**read more about it...
safe sex**

- *And the Bride Wore White: The Seven Secrets to Sexual Purity*
  by Dannah Gresh

- *Boy Meets Girl: Say Hello to Courtship*
  by Josh Harris

- *Diary of a Teenage Girl: Becoming Me*
  by Melody Carlson

- *It's Ok to Say No: Choosing Sexual Abstinence*
  by Eleanor Ayer

- *Passion and Purity*
  by Elisabeth Elliot

- *Wait for Me: Rediscovering the Joy of Purity in Romance*
  by Rebecca St. James

SAFE SEX

THE 1960S WERE known for many rebellions, among them the sexual revolution. Free love spilled from the hippie movement into the mainstream American culture. Premarital sexual relations sanctioned by the new morality became openly flaunted.

> **The Bible** has a word to describe "safe" sex: it's called marriage.
>
> Gary Smalley and John Trent

One of the unexpected results of this trend, however, received little publicity. As reported by Dr. Francis Braceland, past president of the American Psychiatric Association and editor of the American Journal of Psychiatry, an increasing number of young people were admitted to mental hospitals during that time. In discussing this finding at a National Methodist Convocation of Medicine and Theology, Braceland concluded, "A more lenient attitude on campus about premarital sexual experience has imposed stresses on some college women severe enough to cause emotional breakdown."

Looking back over the years since the new morality was sanctioned by a high percentage of the American culture, one finds a rising number of rapes, abortions, divorces, premarital pregnancies, single-family homes, and cases of sexually transmitted diseases, including herpes and HIV.

The evidence is compelling: the old morality produced safer, healthier, and happier people!

Marriage should be honored by all, and the marriage bed kept pure, for God will judge the adulterer and all the sexually immoral.

HEBREWS 13:4 NIV

Facts

George Eastman kept looking until he found the answers to his questions. Can you find the answers to these questions?

1. Why is "abbreviated" such a long word?
2. Why is lemon juice made with artificial flavor, and dishwashing liquid made with real lemons?
3. Why is the man who invests people's money called a broker?
4. Why are they called apart-ments when they are all stuck together?
5. Why isn't there mouse-flavored cat food?
6. Why do doctors call what they do "practice?"
7. Why does the sun lighten your hair, but darken your skin?

LONG-TERM VISION

You must have **long-range goals** to keep you from being frustrated by **short-range** failures.

CHARLES C. NOBLE

In 1877, George Eastman dreamed that the wonderful world of photography might be accessible to the average person. At the time, photographers working outdoors had to carry multiple pieces of bulky equipment and a corrosive agent called silver nitrate. Eastman theorized that if he could eliminate most of this equipment, he would have something.

Working in a bank by day, he spent his nights reading books on chemistry and magazines about photography. He took foreign language lessons so he could read information published in France and Germany. Then with a partner, he began his own company in 1881. Almost immediately, a problem arose with the new dry plates he had invented. Eastman refunded the money to those who had purchased them and returned to his lab. Three months and 472 experiments later, he came up with the durable emulsion for which he had searched!

Eastman spent many nights sleeping in a hammock at his factory after long days designing equipment. To replace the glass used for photographic plates, he created a roll of thin, flexible material now known as film. To replace heavy tripods, he developed a pocket camera. By 1895, photography was at last available for the common man.

George Eastman's long-term vision kept him motivated even when 471 experiments failed. Keeping your ultimate dream in mind, set short, attainable goals; and before you even know it, your vision will be a reality!

Let us fix our eyes on Jesus, the author and perfecter of our faith, who for the joy set before him endured the cross, scorning its shame, and sat down at the right hand of the throne of God.

HEBREWS 12:2 NIV

BUILDING BRIDGES

> PEOPLE ARE LONELY BECAUSE THEY BUILD WALLS INSTEAD OF BRIDGES.
>
> JOSEPH EWTON

A FABLE IS TOLD of a young orphan boy who had no family and no one to love him. Feeling sad and lonely, he was walking through a meadow one day when he saw a small butterfly caught in a thorn bush. The more the butterfly struggled to free itself, the deeper the thorns cut into its fragile body. The boy carefully released the butterfly, but instead of flying away, the butterfly transformed into an angel right before his eyes.

The boy rubbed his eyes in disbelief as the angel said, "For your wonderful kindness, I will do whatever you would like." The little boy thought for a moment and then said, "I want to be happy!" The angel replied, "Very well," and then leaned toward him, whispered in his ear, and vanished.

As the little boy grew up, there was no one in the land as happy as he. When people asked him the secret of his happiness, he would only smile and say, "I listened to an angel when I was a little boy."

On his deathbed, his neighbors rallied around him and asked him to divulge the key to his happiness before he died. The old man finally told them: "The angel told me that everyone, no matter how secure they seemed, no matter how old or young, how rich or poor, had need of me."

You have something to give to everyone you come in contact with today. Build bridges instead of walls!

You should be like one big happy family
. . . loving one another with tender
hearts and humble minds.

1 PETER 3:8 TLB

TOP 10 TIPS

for Tearing Down Walls
and Building Bridges

1. DECIDE TO TAKE THE RISK AND INITIATE A CONVERSATION WITH SOMEONE NEW.

2. PAY A SINCERE COMPLIMENT TO SOMEONE YOU DON'T KNOW.

3. BANISH THE FEAR OF FAMILIARITY.

4. GREET STRANGERS WITH A "GOOD MORNING" AND A SMILE.

5. BE APPROACHABLE; LOOK OTHERS DIRECTLY IN THE EYE AND SMILE.

6. INVITE SOMEONE NEW TO A SCHOOL EVENT.

7. ASK INTERESTED QUESTIONS ABOUT THAT PERSON.

8. BE A GOOD LISTENER.

9. WHEN THE TIME COMES, SHARE ABOUT YOURSELF FREELY AND OPENLY.

10. GIVE OTHERS A CHANCE; THEY ARE PROBABLY JUST AS UNSURE AS YOU ARE.

HOW Do YOU MEASURE Up?

How do you treat your parents?

A. I sometimes disagree with them, but I always show them respect.
B. We disagree often, and I struggle to manage my anger when we fight.
C. They are totally out of line; I can't respect them.
D. I get angry at times, but I usually apologize when I've been out of line.
E. When we disagree, I try to remember that they have more experience than I do. Besides, I know they love me and want the best for me.

The teen years can bring much stress within the family. Teenagers can feel that their parents don't understand them, and parents can feel that their teenagers are inconsiderate and even mean to them. But the Bible is clear. "Honor your father and mother": is the first commandment that has a promise attached to it, namely, "so you will live well and have a long life" (Ephesians 6:1 MSG).

BLESS YOUR PARENTS

CHILDREN WHO BRING HONOR TO THEIR PARENTS REAP BLESSINGS FROM THEIR GOD.

A mother watched with raised eyebrows as her two sons took a hammer and a few nails from the kitchen utility drawer and scurried to one of the boys' rooms, giggling and talking in low voices. When she didn't hear any hammering, she continued with her chores. Then from the kitchen window, she saw one of the boys take a stepladder from the garage. He disappeared from sight before she could call to him. A few minutes later, her other son came into the kitchen to ask if she had any rope. "No," Mom said. "What's going on?" Her son said, "Nothin'." Mom pressed, "Are you sure?" But her son was out of sight.

Highly suspicious, Mom went to her son's room. She found the door closed and locked. She knocked. "What are you boys doing in there?" she asked. One son replied, "Nothin'." Suspecting great mischief, she demanded entrance. "I want you to open this door right now!" she said. A few seconds later, the door popped open, and her son shouted, "Surprise!" as he handed her a rather crudely wrapped present. "Happy birthday, Mom!" the other boy added. Truly surprised, the mother stammered, "But what about the hammer, nails, ladder, and rope?" The boys grinned, "Those were just decoys, Mom."

"Honor your father and your mother, so that you may live long in the land the Lord your God is giving you."

EXODUS 20:12 NIV

YOUR ENEMY IS
ALREADY DEFEATED

Several years ago, a well-known television circus developed an act involving Bengal tigers. The act was performed live before a large audience. One night, the tiger trainer went into the cage with several tigers, and the door was routinely locked behind him. Spotlights flooded the cage, and television cameras moved in close, so the audience could see every detail as he skillfully put the tigers through their paces.

In the middle of the performance, the worst happened: the lights went out. For nearly thirty long seconds, the trainer was locked in with the tigers in the darkness. With their superb night vision, the tigers could see him, but he could not see them. Still, he survived. When the lights came back on, he calmly finished his performance.

When the trainer was asked how he felt, he admitted to feeling chilling fear at first; but then, he said he realized that even though he couldn't see the big cats, they didn't know he couldn't see them. He said, "I just kept cracking my whip and talking to them until the lights came on. They never knew I couldn't see them as well as they could see me."

Keep talking back to the tigers of fear that seem to be stalking you. They will obey your voice of faith!

> COURAGE IS THE MASTERY OF FEAR, NOT THE ABSENCE OF FEAR.
> MARK TWAIN

THOUGH I WALK THROUGH THE VALLEY OF THE SHADOW OF DEATH, I WILL FEAR NO EVIL; FOR YOU ARE WITH ME; YOUR ROD AND YOUR STAFF, THEY COMFORT ME.

PSALM 23:4 NKJV

WISE WORDS

Courage is a special kind of knowledge: the knowledge of how to fear what ought to be feared and how not to fear what ought not to be feared.

BEN GURION

THE BEST ANSWER TO FEAR IS "NO"

A teenager named Buck was walking to his father's apartment from a subway stop one day when he suddenly realized that two men were flanking him.

"Give me your wallet," one of the men insisted. "I have a gun. Give me your wallet, or I'll shoot."

"No," Buck said.

"Hey, man, you don't understand. We're robbing you. Give me your wallet."

"No."

"Give me your wallet, or I'll knife you."

"No."

"Give me your wallet, or we'll beat you up."

By now the robber was pleading more than he was demanding.

"No," Buck said once again. He kept walking, and a few steps later, he realized that the two men had disappeared. As he related this story to a friend, the friend asked, "Weren't you scared?"

Buck replied, "Of course I was scared!"

"Then why didn't you give them your wallet?"

"Because," Buck answered matter-of-factly, "my learner's permit is in it."

While it may be wise to give in to the demands of a thief, the first and best answer to fear is always no!

lighten up

Fear turned to laughter for the victims of these bungled robberies:

° A Connecticut man learned a valuable lesson when robbing banks: Wait until you get home to count the loot. Ernest Michaelson, 45, was discovered behind the bank moments after it had been robbed. Police said Michaelson was counting the stolen money when police arrived and arrested him.

° A bungling crook in Rome, Italy, was arrested after he took a shop dummy hostage. The gun-wielding robber threatened to shoot the lifelike mannequin if the cops made any attempt to capture him. A police spokesman said "He was either blind as a bat, dumb, or both."

Be strong and of good courage . . . for the LORD
DEUTERONOMY 31:6 NKJV

> "One man with courage makes a majority."

your God . . . will not leave you nor forsake you.

CONSIDER THIS!

A scorpion, being a poor swimmer, asked a turtle to carry him on his back across a river. "Are you mad?" exclaimed the turtle. "You'll sting me while I'm swimming, and I'll drown."

"My dear turtle," laughed the scorpion, "if I were to sting you, you would drown, and I would go down with you. Now, where is the logic in that?"

"You're right," cried the turtle. "Hop on!"

The scorpion climbed aboard and halfway across the river gave the turtle a mighty sting. As they both sank to the bottom, the turtle resignedly said, "Do you mind if I ask you something? You said there'd be no logic in your stinging me. Why did you do it?"

"It has nothing to do with logic," the drowning scorpion sadly replied. "It's just my character."

LET YOUR
CHARACTER SHINE

When Chief Justice Charles Evans Hughes moved to Washington, D.C., to take up his duties on the Supreme Court, he transferred his church membership letter to a Baptist church in the area.

It was customary for all new members in this church to come to the front of the sanctuary at the close of the worship service, so they might be officially introduced and welcomed. The first person to be called forward that morning was Ah Sing, a Chinese laundryman who had moved to Washington from the West Coast. He took his place at the far side of the church. As the dozen or so others were called forward that day, they came forward

> **LET US NOT SAY, "EVERY MAN IS THE ARCHITECT OF HIS OWN FORTUNE"; BUT LET US SAY, "EVERY MAN IS THE ARCHITECT OF HIS OWN CHARACTER."**
> **GEORGE DANA BOARDMAN**

and stood on the opposite side of the church, leaving Ah Sing standing alone.

Finally Chief Justice Hughes was called forward, and he immediately made his way to the front and proceeded to stand next to Ah Sing. The minister who welcomed the group into church fellowship said, "I do not want this congregation to miss this remarkable illustration of the fact that at the cross of Jesus Christ, the ground is level."

Your character is shown in many ways, but one of the most obvious is the way you treat people. You will grow in character and reputation if you treat others with kindness.

Till I die I will not put away my integrity from me. My righteousness I hold fast, and will not let it go; my heart shall not reproach me as long as I live.

JOB 27:5-6 NKJV

He who has a slack hand
becomes poor, but the hand
of the diligent makes rich.

PROVERBS 10:4 NKJV

DON'T GIVE UP, WORK HARDER

EARLY IN THE 1989 basketball season, Michigan faced Wisconsin. With just seconds left in the fourth quarter, Michigan's Rumeal Robinson found himself at the foul line. His team was trailing by one point, and he knew that if he could sink both shots, Michigan would win. Sadly, Rumeal missed both shots. Wisconsin upset the favored Michigan, and Rumeal went to the locker room feeling devastated and embarrassed.

His dejection, however, spurred him into action and ignited his determination. He decided that at the end of each practice for the rest of the season, he was going to shoot one hundred extra foul shots. Shoot 'em he did!

The moment came when Rumeal stepped to the foul line in yet another game, again with the opportunity to make two shots. This time, there were only three seconds left in overtime, and the game was the NCAA finals! Swish went the first shot; and swish went the second! Those two points gave Michigan the victory and the Collegiate National Championship for the season.

Have you just failed at something? Don't give up. Instead, work harder. Success is possible!

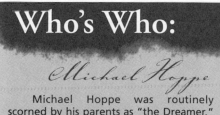

Who's Who:

Michael Hoppe was routinely scorned by his parents as "the Dreamer," because of his desire to compose music. Instead, they encouraged him to become a businessman. Since he was an obedient son, he did just that. In fact, he became a senior executive for one of the world's largest record companies. He brought in many talented composers and artists while quietly composing his own music.

One day, Hoppe played a tape that auditioned his company's talent for a major film producer, but the producer rejected artist after artist. "Don't you have anyone right for me?" he asked. As the tape wound to the end, Hoppe's own music rang out. He realized in horror that he had taped over one of his own compositions and stopped the tape.

"That's it!" cried the producer. "That's our composer!

Since that audition, Michael Hoppe has recorded over a dozen CDs—several reaching gold and platinum levels. Had he stopped working on his own music when he became a businessman, he would never have experienced this success.

THE MOST IMPORTANT PERSON IN YOUR LIFE

When Ruth Bell was a teenager, she was sent from her childhood home in China to school in Korea. At the time, she fully intended to follow in her parents' footsteps and become a missionary. She envisioned herself a confirmed old maid, ministering to the people of Tibet. While at school, however, Ruth did give some serious thought to the kind of husband that she might consider. As she tells in her book *A Time for Remembering*, she listed these particulars:

> **This** explains why a man leaves his father and mother and is joined to his wife, and the two are united into one.
> GENESIS 2:24 NLT

"If I marry: He must be so tall that when he is on his knees, as one has said, he reaches all the way to heaven. His shoulders must be broad enough to bear the burden of a family. His lips must be strong enough to smile, firm enough to say no, and tender enough to kiss. Love must be so deep that it takes its stand in Christ and so wide that it takes the whole lost world in. He must be active enough to save souls. He must be big enough to be gentle and great enough to be thoughtful. His arms must be strong enough to carry a little child."

Ruth Bell never did become a full-time missionary in Tibet. She did, however, find a man worth marrying—Billy Graham. As his wife, Ruth Bell Graham became a missionary to the whole world!

Your spouse will be the most important person in your life. It's crucial to marry the right person. Think about the qualities that you would like to have in a mate. If you haven't already, begin to pray for the person you will eventually marry. Even if you haven't met him or her yet, God knows who he or she is.

You will never **make** a more **important** **decision** than the person you **marry**.

DR. EUGENE SWEARINGEN

#1 **When you marry, your mate will have more influence on you than any other earthly person. A choice of this magnitude deserves your best planning. Below are a few things you can do to prepare for making that choice.**

#2

- Make a list of the qualities you are looking for in a mate.
- Draft a letter to your future mate telling him or her what you appreciate about these qualities.

#3

- Pray for your future mate on a daily basis.
- Write another letter to tell your future mate about something you would not tell anyone else.

#4

- Strive to develop the qualities in your own life that you have listed for your future mate.

#5

fyi booklist

read more about it...
making dreams come true

- **Chocolate for a Teen's Dreams: Heartwarming Stories about Making Your Wishes Come True**
  by Kay Allenbaugh

- *Making Your Dreams Come True*
  by Marcia Wieder

- *Life Strategies for Teens*
  by Jay McGraw

- **I'd Change My Life If I Had More Time: A Practical Guide to Making Dreams Come True**
  by Doreen Virtue

- **When Dreams Come True : A Love Story Only God Could Write**
  by Eric Ludy, Leslie Ludy

- **The Rookie: The Incredible True Story of a Man Who Never Gave Up on His Dream**
  by Jim Morris, Joel Engel

SUCCESS DOESN'T COME BY CHANCE

THE SIXTY-FOUR-THOUSAND-dollar Question was the hottest show on television in 1955. The more Joyce watched the program, the more she thought, "I could do that." At the time, Joyce had quit her teaching job to raise her daughter, and she and her husband were living on fifty dollars a month. She never dreamed of winning the top prize—any prize at that point would have helped greatly.

As a psychologist by training, Joyce analyzed the show. She saw that each contestant had a built-in incongruity—the marine who was a gourmet cook, the shoemaker who knew about opera. She looked at herself. She was a short, blond psychologist and mother with no incongruity. After some thought, she decided to become an expert in boxing! She ate, drank, and slept boxing, studying its statistics, personalities, and history. When she felt she was ready, she applied as a contestant for the show, was accepted, won, and won again, until she eventually won the sixty-four-thousand-dollar prize.

That experience led her to dream of a career as a television journalist who might translate the results of psychological research into terms that people could use in their everyday lives. Once she saw that possibility, there was no stopping Dr. Joyce Brothers.

True success never comes by chance. Diligently apply yourself to your goals, and your dreams will come true.

> **Diligence** is the mother of good fortune.
>
> Cervantes

The plans of the **diligent** lead to **profit**.

PROVERBS 21:5 NIV

HE HEARS EVERY PRAYER

Both a major thoroughfare in Tel Aviv and a bridge that spans the Jordan River are named in honor of Viscount Edmund Henry Hynman Allenby, a British solider. As commander of the Egyptian Expeditionary Forces, he outwitted and defeated the Turks in Palestine in 1917 and 1918, conquering Jerusalem without ever firing a single gun.

As a British solider, Allenby was noncommittal about the official British policies concerning the establishment of a Jewish national home, but he did have a deep understanding of the Jews' desire to dwell in Palestine. At a reception in London, he once told how as a little boy, he had knelt to say his evening prayers, repeating with his childhood lisp the words his mother prayed: "And, O Lord, we would not forget Thine ancient people, Israel; hasten the day when Israel shall again be Thy people and shall be restored to Thy favor and to their land."

Allenby con-cluded, "I never knew then that God would give me the privilege of helping to answer my own childhood prayers."

What you pray today may well be part of tomorrow's work. The world you envision in prayer may well be the world in which you one day will live!

HE WHO IS WAITING FOR SOMETHING TO TURN UP MIGHT START WITH HIS OWN SHIRT-SLEEVES.

WE USE GOD'S MIGHTY WEAPONS, NOT MERE WORLDLY WEAPONS, TO KNOCK DOWN THE DEVIL'S STRONGHOLD.

2 CORINTHIANS 10:4 NLT

WISE WORDS

God is never more than a prayer away from
you. We address and stamp a letter and
send it on its way, confident that it will
reach its destination, but we doubtfully
wonder if our prayers will be heard by an
ever-present God. If laser beams can cut
through mountains, why should we doubt
the power of prayer? Wonderful things can
happen to us when we live expectantly,
believe confidently, and pray affirmatively.
The pulse of prayer is praise. The heart of
prayer is gratitude. The voice of prayer is
obedience. The arm of prayer is service.

WILLIAM A. WARD

CAN YOU CONTROL YOUR TONGUE?

WILLIAM PENN, founding leader of the colony that became Pennsylvania, had these rules for conversation: "Avoid company where it is not profitable or necessary, and in those occasions, speak little, and last. Silence is wisdom where speaking is folly, and always safe. Some are so foolish as to interrupt and anticipate those that speak instead of hearing and thinking before they answer, which is uncivil, as well as silly. If thou thinkest twice before thou speakest once, thou wilt speak twice the better for it. Better to say nothing than not to the purpose. And to speak pertinently, consider both what is fit, and when it is fit, to speak. In all debates, let truth be thy aim, not victory or an unjust interest; and endeavor to gain, rather than to expose, thy antagonist."

> NOT ONLY TO SAY THE RIGHT THING IN THE RIGHT PLACE, BUT FAR MORE DIFFICULT, TO LEAVE UNSAID THE WRONG THING AT THE TEMPTING MOMENT.
>
> BENJAMIN FRANKLIN

A little girl named Mary had come home from a tough day at school. She stretched herself out on the living room sofa to have her own private pity party. She moaned to her mother and brother, "Nobody loves me . . . the whole world hates me!"

Her brother, busily occupied with his Nintendo, hardly looked her way as he passed on this encouraging word: "That's not true, Mary. Some people don't even know you."

Mary, no doubt, was not amused. She probably wished her brother had heeded the advice of William Penn. One of the greatest skills you can develop in life is the ability to control your tongue!

Self-control means controlling the tongue!

A quick retort can ruin everything.

PROVERBS 13:3 TLB

TOP 10 TIPS

for Controlling Your Tongue

1. SPEAK THE TRUTH IN LOVE.

2. MAKE A COMMITMENT TO ELEVATE OTHERS WITH YOUR WORDS.

3. LISTEN MORE OFTEN THAN YOU SPEAK.

4. FOSTER POSITIVE CONVERSATIONS THAT DO NO HARM.

5. DO NOT GOSSIP.

6. NURTURE POSITIVE THOUGHTS; YOUR WORDS WILL FOLLOW SUIT.

7. COUNT TO TEN BEFORE YOU SPEAK.

8. BITE YOUR TONGUE WHEN YOU'RE TEMPTED TO SAY THE WRONG THING.

9. NEVER LASH OUT IN ANGER.

10. LISTEN TO THE SMALL VOICE OF GOD WITHIN YOU.

Fun Facts

Several years ago a large truck became jammed in the Holland Tunnel leading out of New York City. Traffic was backed up for miles as work crews and engineers struggled to free the truck.

An eight-year-old girl was parked in the gridlock with her family. They were headed out of town for a long weekend, and she fidgeted in the backseat, frustrated with the delay. As they sat and waited, the girl finally reached her limit. She shouted out, " Daddy, why don't they just let the air out of the truck's tires?"

Her dad thought about it for a moment, then he got out of the car to ask the engineers if they had tried this idea. They hadn't, but as they considered the idea, they decided to try it. Guess what? It worked.

Sometimes the possibilities are more obvious to the uncluttered mind of a child than to well-educated adults.

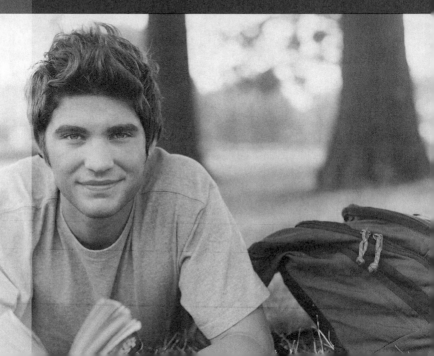

LOOK FOR POSSIBILITIES

The future belongs to those who see possibilities before they become obvious.

JOHN SCULLEY

Eniac was one of the first computers to use electronic circuits, which made for lightning-fast calculations. At first, Thomas J. Watson Jr., the former chairman of IBM, saw no use for it. He said, "I reacted to Eniac the way some people probably reacted to the Wright brothers' airplane. It didn't move me at all. . . . I couldn't see this gigantic, costly, unreliable device as a piece of business equipment."

A few weeks later, he and his father wandered into a research office at IBM and saw an engineer with a high-speed punch-card machine hooked up to a black box. When asked what he was doing, he said, "Multiplying with radio tubes." The machine was tabulating a payroll at one-tenth the time it took the standard punch-card machine to do so. Watson recalls, "That impressed me as though somebody had hit me on the head with a hammer." He said, "Dad, we should put this thing on the market! Even if we only sell eight or ten, we'll be able to advertise the fact that we have the world's first commercial electronic calculator."

That's how IBM got into electronics. Within a year, they had electronic circuits that both multiplied and divided; and at that point, electronic calculators became truly useful. Thousands of the IBM 604 were sold.

What wasn't yet obvious to Thomas Watson was obvious to the engineer working in the research department. Always keep your eyes and ears open; you never know what you might discover. Look for the possibilities around you.

"The vision is yet for an appointed time.

. . . It will surely come, it will not tarry."

HABAKKUK 2:3 NKJV

CONSIDER THIS!

Consider these words by wealthy people:

• "All my possessions are for a moment of time."
Elizabeth I, the Queen of England
• "It is easier to renounce worldly possessions than
it is to renounce the love of them."
Walter Hilton
• And then from the great King Solomon—arguably
the richest man who ever lived: "The lover of
money will not be satisfied with money; nor the
lover of wealth, with gain. This also is vanity."
Ecclesiastes 5:10 NRSV

It's easy to think that we'll be happy as soon as we
get the newest thing every teen is longing for. It
makes us feel like a winner, one of the crowd. But
possessions can't provide happiness and well being.
We may feel great when we first get that special
thing we've been longing for, but that lasts only
until the next great thing comes along. Don't be
fooled into chasing after or hording earthly
possessions. In the end, they mean nothing.

THE SOURCE OF FULFILLMENT

A young man once came to Jesus, asking Him what he needed to do to have eternal life. Jesus replied that he should keep the commandments. The young man then claimed that he had always kept them. Jesus advised, If you would be perfect, sell everything you have, give the money to the poor, and come and follow me. (Matthew 19:21.)

The Scriptures tell us that the young man went away sorrowful: for he had great possessions (v. 22). The young man not only had great possessions, but apparently those possessions had him! He couldn't bear to part with earthly, temporary goods in order to obtain heavenly, eternal goods. Jesus also taught, of course, that Heaven's wealth can be ours now. This young man didn't have to wait until he died to attain the benefits of eternal life. If he had been willing to give up his hold on his stuff, he could have enjoyed great joy, peace, and fulfillment in life—things he was apparently lacking or he wouldn't have asked Jesus the question.

Take a look at your possessions today. Are there books, tapes, or clothes you can give away to someone in need of learning, inspiration, or clothing? Discover how rewarding giving can be!

> **PEOPLE, PLACES, AND THINGS WERE NEVER MEANT TO GIVE US LIFE. GOD ALONE IS THE AUTHOR OF A FULFILLING LIFE.**
>
> GARY SMALLEY AND JOHN TRENT

"I have come that they may have life, and that they may have it more abundantly."

JOHN 10:10 NKJV

COURTESY MAKES EVERYTHING SWEETER

WHICH VIRTUOUS behaviors on earth will still be required in Heaven?

Courage? No. There will be nothing to fear in Heaven. Hope? No. We will have all that we desire.

Faith? No. We will be in the presence of the Source of our faith, and all those things for which we have believed will have their fulfillment in Him and by His hand.

Acts of charity toward those in need? No. There will be no hunger, thirst, nakedness, or homelessness in Heaven. All needs will be supplied.

Sympathy? No, for there will be no more tears and no more pain.

Kindness and gratitude? Yes! There will still be room for showing kindness to others, for being grateful for the kindnesses others have shown us.

Kindness puts people at ease, which in turn makes them more cooperative and happy. Immanuel Kant once said, "Always treat a human being as a person, that is, as an end in himself, and not merely as a means to your end." Strive to impart dignity and self-worth to all you meet. Consider it dress rehearsal for your future life in Heaven!

{ **Two Incredibly** Powerful Words: "Thank You." }

Jesus said, "Treat others the same way you want them to treat you."

LUKE 6:31 NASB

A new family moved to our area and began attending our church. They have a teenage boy who attends our youth group. A lot of the kids in our group just ignore him because he acts kind of different. I don't know if he's just shy and awkward or if there is something wrong with him. I want to be friendly, but I'm not sure what to do. Can you help me?

It's good that you have noticed the stray lamb in the flock. You have a sensitive spirit. There are a few things that we all respond to, regardless of our personality differences. Among those things is kindness, consideration, respect, and attention.

• Kindness doesn't cost a cent, yet its value is too great to be calculated.

• Consideration is something we all appreciate receiving.

• Respect is something we all deserve to receive.

• Attention will gently build a bridge of friendship.

Try to find opportunities to show this new boy that he can count on you for kindness, consideration, respect, and attention. He will soon begin to feel more welcome. Also, you will set an example for the rest of the kids in your group. You may be surprised to find them following suit.

In everyday life, how do you reach out to others?

A. I offer to help at home, even when I'm not asked
   to help.
B.) If I reach the lunch line at the same time as another
   student, I allow that student to go first.
C. I offer to do something nice for my brother or sister.
D. When one of my friends asks me for a favor, I try to
   accommodate.
E. When I'm asked to do my chores, I do them quickly
   because I'm a vital part of the teamwork that makes
   my family work.

The teen years can bring a growing awareness of others, a time to become less self-centered and focus on considering other people's needs. Look over your answers again and ask yourself if you reach out to others in the same way you would like them to reach out to you.

DO IT FOR OTHERS

WHEN YOU ARE LABORING FOR OTHERS LET IT BE WITH THE SAME ZEAL AS IF IT WERE FOR YOURSELF.

On May 21, 1946, a scientist at Los Alamos was carrying out a necessary experiment in preparation for an atomic test to be conducted in the waters of the South Pacific. He had successfully performed this experiment many times before. It involved pushing two hemispheres of uranium together to determine the amount of U-235 needed for a chain reaction—the amount scientists call "a critical mass." Just as the mass became critical, he would push the hemispheres apart with his screwdriver, in-stantly stopping the chain reaction.

That day, however, just as the material became critical, the screwdriver slipped. The hemispheres of uranium came too close together, and instantly the room was filled with a dazzling bluish haze. Young Louis Soltin, instead of ducking and thereby possibly saving himself, tore the two hemispheres apart with his hands, thus interrupting the chain reaction.

In this instant, self-forgetful act, he saved the lives of seven other people who were in the room. He, however, died in agony nine days later.

Today, do something for someone else with the same ener-gy you would use if you were doing it for yourself.

Each of you should look not only to your own interests, but also to the interests of others.

PHILIPPIANS 2:4 NIV

SERVING OTHERS IS PRECIOUS TO GOD

Lord of all pots and pans and things,
Since I've no time to be
A saint by doing lovely things,
Or watching late with Thee,
Or dreaming in the dawnlight,
Or storming heaven's gates,
Make me a saint by getting meals,
And washing up the plates.
Although I have Martha's hands,
I have a Mary's mind;
And when I black the boots and shoes,
Thy sandals, Lord, I find.
I think of how they trod the earth,
Each time I scrub the floor.
Accept this meditation, Lord,
I haven't time for more.
Warm all the kitchen with Thy love,
And light it with Thy peace;
Forgive me all my worrying,
And make all grumbling cease.
Thou who didst love to give men food,
In a room or by the sea,
Accept this service that I do—
I do it unto Thee.
—Unknown

JESUS SAID, "THE MORE LOWLY YOUR SERVICE
TO OTHERS, THE GREATER YOU ARE.
TO BE THE GREATEST, BE A SERVANT."

MATTHEW 23:11 TLB

WISE WORDS

Always keep your eyes open for the little task, because it is the little task that is important to Jesus Christ. The future of the kingdom of God does not depend on the enthusiasm of this or that powerful person; those great ones are necessary too, but it is equally necessary to have a great number of little people who will do a little thing in the service of Christ.

ALBERT SCHWEITZER

Service is nothing but
love in work clothes.

"You are never so **HIGH** as when you are on your knees."

JEAN HODGES

> **O my son, be wise and stay in God's paths.**
>
> PROVERBS 23:19 TLB

ASK GOD TO OPEN YOUR EYES

MANY YEARS AGO IN South Africa, a man sold his farm so that he might spend his days in search of diamonds. He was consumed with dreams of becoming wealthy. When he had finally exhausted his resources and his health and was no closer to his fortune than the day he sold his farm, he threw himself into a river and drowned.

One day, the man who had bought his farm spotted an unusual-looking stone in a creek bed. He placed it on his fireplace mantle as a conversation piece. A visitor noticed the stone and examined it closely. He then voiced his suspicion that the stone was actually a diamond. The discreet farmer had the stone analyzed, and sure enough, it was one of the largest and finest diamonds ever found.

Still operating with great secrecy, the farmer searched his stream, gathering similar stones. They were all diamonds. In fact, his farm was covered with diamonds just waiting to be picked up! The farm the diamond-seeker had sold turned out to be one of the richest diamond deposits in the world.

The lessons of wisdom can often be learned in the relationships and experiences we encounter every day. Ask God to reveal to you what you need to know in order to live the life He desires. The resources you need are probably right in front of you.

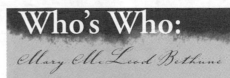

Who's Who:
Mary McLeod Bethune

Mary McLeod Bethune was born one of seventeen children to freed slaves following the end of the Civil War. Mary dreamed of going to Africa as a missionary to teach poor black children. She attended Moody Bible Institute to prepare herself for that dream, but after graduation, she could not find a mission board that would support her vision.

Her disappointment threatened to overwhelm her, and she wondered why God would call her to do something that seemed impossible for her. "If not Africa, then where?" Mary prayed.

In 1904, a Methodist minister told Mary about impoverished Black railroad laborers in Florida. In their struggle to survive, an education for their children was not even a consideration.

Mary learned a lesson about being a missionary. She discovered that you don't have to travel halfway around the world to launch a mission. Sometimes it lies just outside your own back door.

Read more in your public library about the extraordinary legacy that Mary left African Americans.

booklist

read more about it...
positive thinking

- **The Power of Positive Thinking for Teens**
by Mary Lou Carney, Norman Vincent Peale

- **Positive Thinking Every Day : An Inspiration for Each Day of the Year**
by Dr. Norman Vincent Peale

- **The 7 Habits of Highly Effective Teens**
by Sean Covey

- **Learned Optimism: How to Change Your Mind and Your Life**
by Martin Seligman

SEE THE POSSIBILITIES

A NUMBER OF YEARS ago the John Hancock Mutual Life Insurance Company ran an ad that said:

"There was once a man who loved nature with such a deep and moving love that she told him one of her secrets. She gave him the power to create new plants. The man, whose name was Luther Burbank, . . . saw that every plant was a child. It had its own face, own promise, its unique touch of genius or character. And if that promise were tended and encouraged, the plant would grow more useful and beautiful each year. Luther Burbank . . . made potatoes grow larger, whiter, more delicious than they had ever been. He taught the cactus of the desert to throw away its spines, so that cattle could fatten upon it, and made the blackberry shed its thorns, so it would not cut the fingers of the pickers. For him, the plum grew without pits, and strawberries ripened all year . . . . he left the earth covered with flowers and fruits that no one had ever attempted to grow before. And all because he knew a secret. He knew that everything that lives has the power to become greater."

Choose to see new possibilities. Put your mind to them. Let them be the focus of your thoughts, and then pursue them! You will become greater for it.

> **Here's** the key to success and the key to failure: we become what we think about.
> Earl Nightingale

Summing it all up, friends, I'd say you'll do best by filling your minds and meditating on things true, noble, reputable, authentic, compelling, gracious—the best, not the worst; the beautiful, not the ugly; things to praise, not things to curse.

PHILIPPIANS 4:8 MSG

CONSIDER THIS!

Have you taken the opportunity of committing your life to Christ? If not, now is the time. Don't put it off any longer; start living life anew today. It's simple. Just say, "Lord Jesus, thank You for dying for me on the cross. Forgive me of my sins and come into my heart."

If you prayed that prayer, the Bible tells us that you are a new creature. It's time to celebrate! Begin by telling others what you have done. Your family should be first, and don't forget to also call your friends and let them know. If you go to church, let your pastor know.

IT'S THE COURTEOUS THING TO DO

The letters RSVP stand for the French phrase réspondéz s'il vous plaît. . .or, "please respond." This phrase on an invitation asks that you let the host or hostess know whether you plan to attend the function. Every invitation marked with RSVP requires that you call or write the host to let them know that you either will or will not be there.

Occasionally, a handwritten invitation will say, "RSVP, regrets only." In this case, you are required to notify the host only if you will not be attending. A truly thoughtful guest who plans to attend, however, will call or mail a note to the host to thank them for the invitation and to confirm that he or she will attend.

HE WHO CREATED US WITHOUT OUR HELP WILL NOT SAVE US WITHOUT OUR CONSENT.

SAINT AUGUSTINE

Imagine that you planned a catered party for fifty guests and you were paying twenty-five dollars per guest. Then imagine that half your guests failed to respond, and ten of them did not show up. You would be spending two hundred and fifty dollars for people who simply were not considerate enough to let you know that they could not be present. Would you consider those people to be thoughtful friends?

The most important RSVP in all of life is our response to God's invitation to spend eternity with Him in Heaven. Have you sent your RSVP?

If you **confess** with your **mouth,** "**Jesus** is **Lord,**" and **believe** in your **heart** that **God raised** him from the **dead,** you will be **saved.**

ROMANS 10:9 NIV

BRING YOUR DREAMS TO LIFE

In 1972, *Life* magazine published a story about the amazing adventures of John Goddard. When he was fifteen, John's grandmother said, "If only I had done that when I was young. . . ." Determined not to make that statement at the end of his life, John wrote out 127 goals for his life.

He named ten rivers he wanted to explore and seventeen mountains he wanted to climb. He set goals of becoming an Eagle Scout, a world traveler, and a pilot. Also on his list was: ride a horse in the Rose Bowl parade, dive in a submarine, retrace the travels of Marco Polo, read the Bible from cover to cover, and read the entire Encyclopedia Britannica.

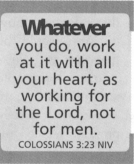

Whatever you do, work at it with all your heart, as working for the Lord, not for men.
COLOSSIANS 3:23 NIV

He also planned to read the entire works of Shakespeare, Plato, Dickens, Socrates, Aristotle, and several other classic authors. He desired to learn to play the flute and violin, marry, have children (he had five), pursue a career in medicine, and serve as a missionary for his church.

Sound impossible? At the age of forty-seven, John Goddard had accomplished one hundred and three of his goals!

Your list of goals may not be as extensive as John Goddard's, but if you don't have some goals in life, you'll find that you have little motivation to get up in the morning and little satisfaction as your head hits the pillow each night.

Motivation is when your **dreams** put on **work** clothes.

BENJAMIN FRANKLIN

JUST DO IT

#1 Amazingly, most people live a mediocre life, never pursuing the dreams they hold in their hearts. Is it because they don't believe in the possibility of their dreams becoming reality and they lack the courage to try? Whatever the reason, don't **#2** be one of them!

God places dreams inside each one of us. These dreams give us passion for life and help us fulfill our destiny on Earth. **#3** God's plan for you may very well reveal itself while you are pursuing your dreams. Don't settle for mediocrity. You were created for greatness! Have faith and courage and risk it all! Nurture your dreams. Take the steps necessary to make them **#4** a reality. They are God-given and will bring blessing to your life.

This week draft a letter to yourself, list- **#5** ing your dreams and the steps toward making them a reality. Mail the letter to yourself, along with a promise to pursue fulfilling those dreams. Just **#6** do it! Don't ever allow fear to make you settle for mediocrity. God has good plans for your future.

#7

#8

#9

#10

Fun Facts

Edison tried more than 200 different substances in attempting to find a filament for his incandescent bulb. Someone once said to him, "You have failed more than 200 times; why don't you give up?"

His answer was, "Not at all. I have discovered more than 200 things that will not work. I will soon find one that will."

HE WILL WALK WITH YOU

There is **no poverty** that can overtake **diligence**.

JAPANESE PROVERB

A young reporter once interviewed a successful businessman. The reporter asked the man to give him a detailed history of his company. As the man talked at length, the reporter began to be amazed at the enormity of the many problems the man had overcome. He finally asked him, "But how did you overcome so many problems of such great magnitude?"

The old gentleman leaned back in his chair and said, "There's really no trick to it." Then he added, "You know . . . there are some troubles that seem so high you can't climb over them." The reporter nodded in agreement, thinking of several he was currently facing. "And," the wise businessman went on, "there are some troubles so wide you can't walk around them." Again, the reporter nodded. The man went on, raising his voice dramatically, "And there are some problems so deep you can't dig under them." Eager for a solution, the reporter said, "Yes? Yes?"

"It's then," the man concluded, "that you know the only way to beat the problem is to duck your head and wade right through it."

A problem rarely decreases in size while a person stands and stares at it; but when you diligently pursue a solution, your problem is guaranteed to shrink.

Lazy hands make a man
poor, but diligent hands
bring wealth.

PROVERBS 10:4 NIV

BEING ABLE TO YIELD IS A SIGN OF STRENGTH

While driving down a country road, a man came to a very narrow bridge. In front of the bridge, there was a sign that read, "Yield." Seeing no oncoming cars, the man continued across the bridge and to his destination. On his way back this same route, he came to the same one-lane bridge, now from the opposite direction. To his surprise, he saw another "Yield" sign posted there.

Curious, he thought, *I'm sure there was one positioned on the other side.* Sure enough, when he reached the other side of the bridge and looked back, he saw the sign. Yield signs had been placed at both ends of the bridge, obviously with the intent that drivers from both directions were requested to give each other the right-of-way. It was a reasonable and doubly sure way to prevent a head-on collision.

THOSE WHO DESIRE TO LEAD MUST FIRST LEARN TO RESPECT AUTHORITY AND OBEY.

If you find yourself in a combative situation with someone who has more authority than you—or equal authority—it is always wise to yield to them. If they indeed have more authority, a lack of submission will put you in a position to be punished or reprimanded. If you are of equal authority, an exercise of your power will only build resentment in a person better kept as an ally. As the Bible says, we are to prefer one another. (Romans 12:10.)

SHOW RESPECT FOR EVERYONE. LOVE CHRISTIANS EVERY- WHERE. FEAR GOD AND HONOR THE GOVERNMENT.

1 PETER 2:17 TLB

WISE WORDS

If you wish others to respect you, you must show respect for them. For twenty days, approach everyone you meet, irrespective of his station in life, as if he or she were the most important person in the world. Everyone wants to feel that he counts for something and is important to someone. Invariably, people will give their love, respect, and attention to the person who fills that need. Consideration for others generally reflects faith in self and faith in others.

ARI KIEV

ALWAYS LEAVE THEM WANTING MORE

MR. BROWN WAS IN his final year of seminary, preparing to become a pastor. The policy of his school called for him to be available at a moment's notice to fill in for local churches who might need a preacher. Mr. Brown eagerly awaited such an opportunity, and at long last, his moment arrived. The pastor of a country church was called away on an emergency, and Mr. Brown was asked to fill the pulpit.

Having waited so long for the opportunity and having so much to say, Mr. Brown soon became completely immersed in his own words. The more he preached, the more he became inspired to preach. When he glanced at his watch, he was shocked to see that he had preached for a full hour. He was truly embarrassed since he had been allotted only thirty minutes to preach. Knowing that he had preached well into the lunch hour, he made a heartfelt apology to the congregation and sat down.

A young woman hurried to him after the service ended. Obviously more impressed with his personality and appearance—and perhaps his availability—than she was with his message, she gushed, "Oh, Brother Brown, you needn't have apologized. You really didn't talk long—it just seemed long."

The old rule of thumb is, "Always leave them wanting more."

lighten up

An elderly pastor admits to his parishioners that he's feeling lonely. One of them suggests that he buy a pet, so the pastor buys a parrot. After arriving home, the parrot starts swearing at the pastor. Frustrated, the pastor walks up to the parrot, slaps him on the beak, and yells, "QUIT IT!" But this only aggravates the problem.

"All right, that's it" yells the pastor and throws a blanket over the parrot's cage. "BE QUIET!" he screams. But the parrot continues to spew insults.

By now the pastor is so infuriated that he throws the parrot into the freezer, and the parrot becomes very quiet. The pastor gets worried and throws open the freezer door. The parrot climbs out of the freezer, flaps the ice off his wings, and says, "Awfully sorry about the trouble I've caused. In the future, I'll do my best to control my temper. "The parrot paused for a moment, then asked, "Um . . . by the way, what did the chicken do?"

"God has given man one tongue but two ears that we may hear twice as much as we speak."

HOW Do YOU MEASURE Up?

How resilient are you? When you pursue your dreams and nothing happens—or worse yet, your efforts seem thwarted and rejected—how do you respond?

A. I have to back off for a while until I can regroup. Then I try again.
B. I become even more determined to make my dream come true. I keep working at it.
C. I pause and rethink my efforts, asking myself if there is a better way to approach the situation.

Actually, if you do any or all of the above, give yourself an AAA+! There is merit in each of these three responses. Some personalities need to back off and regroup, re-energize, and rethink. In fact, the creative process requires it. It has been said that if you have only three solutions to a situation, then you have not discovered the right solution yet. Keep brainstorming new ideas and innovative solutions. God is the author of creativity. He has built a creative spirit inside each one of us. It is a part of our nature.

Read more on the creative process in the hilariously fun books *A Whack on the Side of the Head* and *A Kick in the Seat of the Pants* by Roger von Oech.

KEEP REACHING

THE RIPEST PEACH IS HIGHEST ON THE TREE.

JAMES WHITCOMB RILEY

McCormick's father was what many might call a tinkerer. A mechanical genius, he invented many farm devices. Sadly, however, he became the laughingstock of his community for attempting to make a grain-cutting device. For years, he worked on the project but never succeeded in getting it to operate reliably.

In spite of the discouragement his father experienced and the continuing ridicule of neighbors, young McCormick took up the old machine as his own proj-ect. He also experienced years of experimentation and failure. Then one day, he succeeded in constructing a reaper that would harvest grain.

Even so, jealous opposition prevented the invention from being used for a number of years. McCormick was able to make sales only after he gave a personal guarantee to each purchaser that the reaper would do the job he claimed it could do. Finally, after decades of trial and error, hoping and waiting, a firm in Cincinnati agreed to manufacture one hundred machines, and the famous McCormick reaper was born.

To get to the ripest peach on the highest branch, you need to climb one limb at a time and not be defeated by the scrape of bark, the occasional fall, and the frequent feeling of being left dangling!

Let us **not** become **weary** in doing **good,** for at the **proper time** we will **reap** a harvest if we **do not** give up.

GALATIANS 6:9 NIV

TREAT IT AS THOUGH IT WERE YOURS

A STORE ONCE HAD THIS layaway policy: "We hold it in the store while you pay for it. You're mad. You take it from the store, and you don't pay for it. We're mad. Better that you're mad." Mark Twain's neighbor may have had this policy in mind when Twain asked to borrow a certain book he had spotted in his neighbor's library. "Why, yes, Mr. Clemens, you're more than welcome to it," the neighbor said. "But I must ask you to read it here. You know I make it a rule never to let any book go out of my library."

Several days later, the neighbor came to Twain's house and asked if he could borrow his lawn mower since his had been taken to the repair shop. "Why, certainly," the humorist replied. "You're more than welcome to it. But I must ask you to use it only in my yard. You know I make it a rule."

Treat what you borrow as if it were a prized possession, returning it promptly. If something happens to it while it is in your possession, make repairs or replace it—not to your satisfaction but to the satisfaction of the owner. Always remember, while the item is in your hands, it is not yours. It still belongs to the other person.

{ **Before you** borrow money from a friend, decide which you need more. }

If a man **borrows** an animal **from** his **neighbor** and it is injured or dies while the **owner** is not present, he must make **restitution**.

EXODUS 22:14 NIV

I borrowed my friend's algebra book to study for a test because I had lost mine at an after-school game. I left it on the floor of my bedroom, and my dog chewed the corner off of it. I'm freaking out because my mom is going to make me pay for it out of my allowance. Is it fair for her to make me pay for it? It was the dog who ruined it.

When you borrowed your friend's book, you became responsible for it. It may not seem fair, but you owe your friend a new book. You see, borrowing is an action that has an unspoken but implied guarantee. Your friend promised to let you use his or her property, and you promised to return it in the same condition you received it. That is what you owe her. So swallow hard and cough up the bucks for the new book. That's what is right, which is not always what is easy, but it is what pleases God. Oh, and one more thing. What would be your response to this situation if it were her dog that bit the corner off of your book?

CONSIDER THIS!

How Do You Spell Contribution?

Consider your assets.

Overcome your weaknesses through practice.

Never allow difficulties to make you despair.

Trust that God has a plan for your life.

Remind yourself of others who have experienced limitations yet succeeded.

If plan "A" doesn't work, go on to plan "B."

Bring your whole self to your endeavors.

Utilize the wisdom and instruction of others.

Trust in the eventual rewards of your hard work.

Instruct yourself in the skills of life.

Override negative thoughts with positive affirmations.

No excuses!

RISE ABOVE YOUR LIMITATIONS

Helen Keller overcame the most difficult of physical challenges to become one of the greatest Americans of the twentieth century. As the result of a fever when she was a baby, Helen was left deaf, blind, and unable to speak. Eventually, with dedication, she learned to communicate with Braille; and her life became an inspiration for millions of people, including Mark Twain, an ardent admirer. She was invited to visit every U.S. President during her lifetime.

As a teenager, she struggled to achieve, finally graduating with honors from Radcliffe College. She wrote numerous articles, gave lectures for the American Foun-dation for the Blind, and raised more than two million dollars for the foundation's work. On her eighti-

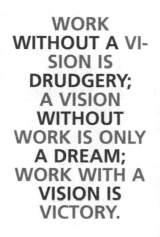

WORK WITHOUT A VISION IS DRUDGERY; A VISION WITHOUT WORK IS ONLY A DREAM; WORK WITH A VISION IS VICTORY.

eth birthday, the American Foundation for Overseas Blind honored her by announcing the Helen Keller International Award for those who give outstanding help to the blind.

Sometimes as young adults, we think there are too many strikes against us—our lives are just too hard. Yet Helen rose above her limitations to make a lasting contribution to our society. Not only are we called to overcome our faults and weaknesses, but we are asked to exercise our strengths. We are challenged to do more than just survive in this world. God desires that we set our minds, hearts, and energy to the work He has planned for us. He's given you the talent to make your dreams a reality.

Work hard so God can say to you, "Well done."

Be a good workman, one who does not need to be ashamed when God examines your work.

2 TIMOTHY 2:15 TLB

GROW INTO YOUR FULL POTENTIAL

ANDREW Carnegie, considered to be one of the first to emphasize self-esteem and the potential for inner greatness, was famous for his ability to produce millionaires from among his employees. One day a reporter asked him, "How do you account for the fact you have forty-three millionaires working for you?"

Carnegie replied, "They weren't rich when they came. We work with people the same way you mine gold. You have to remove a lot of dirt before you find a small amount of gold."

Andrew Carnegie knew how to bring about change in people. He helped them realize their hidden treasure within, inspired

> **EVERYONE THINKS OF CHANGING THE WORLD, BUT NO ONE THINKS OF CHANGING HIMSELF.**
>
> LEO TOLSTOY

them to develop it, and then watched with encouragement as their lives were transformed.

The philosopher and psychologist William James once said, "Compared to what we ought to be, we are only half awake. We are making use of only a small part of our physical and mental resources. Stating the thing broadly, the human individual thus lives far within his limits. He possesses powers of various sorts which he habitually fails to use."

In other words, most people only develop a fraction of their abilities. Go for a bigger percentage in your life. Find the gold within!

Jesus said, "Unless you change and become like little children, you will never enter the kingdom of heaven."

MATTHEW 18:3 NIV

TOP 10 TIPS

fot "Mining" the Hidden "Gold" Within

1. SIFT OFF THE DIRT AND DEBRIS—THE SIN IN YOUR LIFE.

2. REMOVE THE THINGS FROM YOUR LIFE THAT CONTINUALLY POUR MORE DIRT OVER THE GOLD.

3. APPLY WATER—THE BLOOD OF CHRIST'S FORGIVENESS—TO WASH THE GOLD AND REVEAL ITS SHINE.

4. DISCOVER YOUR HIDDEN TREASURE. MAKE A LIST OF YOUR NATURAL GIFTS.

5. TAKE ALL OF YOUR RESOURCES WITH YOU. YOU WILL NEED THEM.

6. TAKE YOUR MAP—THE WORD OF GOD—TO NAVIGATE YOUR JOURNEY.

7. COMMIT TO NOT TURNING BACK UNTIL YOU HAVE FOUND YOUR TREASURE.

8. DON'T FORGET TO ALWAYS TAKE YOUR GUIDE—THE HOLY SPIRIT.

9. BE PREPARED FOR A FEW TREACHEROUS PATHS. THIS IS UNCHARTED TERRITORY.

10. NEVER GIVE UP! NEVER GIVE UP! NEVER GIVE UP!

Whatever your hand finds to do, do it with your might.

ECCLESIASTES 9:10 NKJV

**Triumph is just "umph"
added to try.**

YOU CAN TRIUMPH

MANY YEARS AGO IN England, a small boy grew up speaking with a lisp. He was never a scholar in school. When war broke out involving his nation, he was rejected from service, told that "we need men." He once rose to address the House of Commons, and all present walked out of the room. In fact, he often spoke to empty chairs and echoes. One day, he became Prime Minister of Great Britain; and with stirring speeches and bold decisions, he led his nation to victory. His name was Sir Winston Churchill.

Many years ago in Illinois, a man with only a few years of formal education failed in business in '31, was defeated in a run for the state legislature in '32, again failed in business in '33, was elected to the legislature in '34, but was defeated for speaker in '38. He was defeated for elector in '40, defeated for Congress in '43, elected to Congress in '46, but

defeated in '48. He was defeated for Senate in '55, defeated for the vice-presidential nomination in '56, and defeated for the Senate in '58. In 1860, however, he was elected president. His name was Abraham Lincoln.

No one is defeated until he gives up trying.

Who's Who:

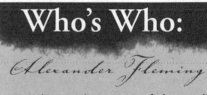

Alexander Fleming

History gives most of the credit for the revolutionary drug, penicillin, to Alexander Fleming, a Scottish scientist who first noticed the powerful anti-bacterial effects of a fungus growing in his laboratory in 1928; the reality is that penicillin would have remained a scientific curiosity had it not been for the ingenuity and tenacity of a group of scientists at Oxford University led by Howard Florey, an indomitable Australian.

Working in the shadow of World War II and often short of funds, the Oxford scientists planned how to save their research should the Nazis invade Britain. Their plan was quite remarkable. They would sow spores of penicillin-producing fungus in their clothing, and then carry their work literally on their backs to safer shores.

SMALL COURTESIES SPEAK VOLUMES

There's an old saying that goes, "It needs more skill than I can tell, to play the second fiddle well."

Along that line, Leonard Bernstein was once asked which instrument was the most difficult to play. He thought for a moment and said, "The second fiddle. I can get plenty of first violinists, but to find someone who can play the second fiddle with enthusiasm—that's a problem. And if we have no second fiddle, we have no harmony."

General Robert E. Lee was a man who knew the value of playing second fiddle. This great general never stopped being a true southern gentleman. Once, while riding on a train to Richmond, he was seated at the rear of the car. All the other places were filled with officers and soldiers. A poorly dressed, elderly woman boarded the coach at a rural station, and finding no seat offered to her, she trudged down the aisle toward the back of the car. Immediately, Lee stood up and offered her his place. One after another of the men then arose and offered the general his seat. "No, gentlemen," he replied, "if there is none for this lady, there can be none for me!"

Genuine humility is what prompts us to offer a heartfelt thank you and to favor others over ourselves.

THE TWO MOST IMPORTANT WORDS: "THANK YOU." THE MOST IMPORTANT WORD: "WE." THE LEAST IMPORTANT WORD: "I."

BUILDER

DON'T BE SELFISH. . . . BE HUMBLE, THINKING OF OTHERS AS BETTER THAN YOURSELF.

PHILIPPIANS 2:3 TLB

WISE WORDS

Jesus said, "You have heard that the law of Moses says, 'If an eye is injured, injure the eye of the person who did it. If a tooth gets knocked out, knock out the tooth of the person who did it.' But I say, don't resist an evil person! If you are slapped on the right cheek, turn the other, too. If you are ordered to court and your shirt is taken from you, give your coat, too. If a soldier demands that you carry his gear for a mile, carry it two miles. Give to those who ask, and don't turn away from those who want to borrow.

"You have heard that the law of Moses says, 'Love your neighbor' and hate your enemy. But I say, love your enemies! Pray for those who persecute you! In that way, you will be acting as true children of your Father in heaven. For he gives his sunlight to both the evil and the good, and he sends rain on the just and on the unjust, too. If you love only those who love you, what good is that? Even corrupt tax collectors do that much.

MATTHEW 5:38-46 NLT

booklist

read more about it...teen issues

- *Teen Love: On Friendship (Chicken Soup for the Teenage Soul)*
  by Kimberly Kirberger

- *Things Get Hectic: Teens Write about the Violence that Surrounds Them*
  by Youth Communication, et al

- *Closing the Gap: A Strategy For Bringing Parents And Teens Together*
  by Jay McGraw

- *Always Accept Me for Who I Am : Instructions from Teenagers on Raising the Perfect Parent by 147 Teens Who Know*
  by J. S. Salt

- *The 7 Habits of Highly Effective Teens*
  by Sean Covey

PAY ATTENTION

HENRY P. DAVISON WAS a prominent American financier and one-time head of the American Red Cross. He worked his way up from being a poor boy to become president of a large New York City bank.

While he was a cashier of that bank, a would-be robber came to his window, pointed a revolver at him, and passed a check across his window counter. The check was for one million dollars, payable to the Almighty. Davison remained calm, even though he realized the gravity of the situation. In a loud voice, he repeated the words on the check back to the person standing in front of him, emphasizing the "million dollars." Then he graciously asked the would-be rob-

> **I think** the one lesson I have learned is that there is no substitute for paying attention.
> — Diane Sawyer

ber how he would like to have the million dollars for the Almighty. He then proceeded to count out small bills. In the meantime, the suspicion of a guard had been aroused by the strange request he had overheard. He disarmed the robber and prevented the theft.

In later years, Davison was often asked to give his wisdom to others seeking success. He often advised that courtesy, readiness, willingness, and alertness do more for a person than just being smart.

It has been said that one of the skills of a good communicator is the ability to listen. Paying attention to the words and actions of those around you may be the best schooling you'll ever receive.

We must **listen** very **carefully** to the **truth** we have **heard,** or we may drift away from it.

HEBREWS 2:1 NLT

Fun Facts

Once upon a time, a man went on a long trip to visit his friend, carrying a swan as a gift for his host. Unfortunately, the swan escaped from the cage on the way. The man was able to take hold of the swan as it was escaping, but his effort produced nothing more than a feather. Having lost his gift, the man could have returned home. Instead, he continued his journey with the swan feather in hand. When the man presented the feather to his friend, he happily received this unexpected gift, deeply moved by the story as well as the sincerity. The incident is said to have inspired the saying "the gift is nothing much, but it's the thought that counts." This story comes from China where showing courtesy is considered to be an important part of a person's character. Surely God expects us to treat our friends with the same degree of thoughtfulness and care.

UNCOMMON COURTESIES

Nothing is ever lost by **courtesy**. . . . It **pleases** him who gives and him who **receives**, and thus, like **mercy**, it is twice **blessed**.

ERASTUS WIMAN

We often refer to courtesy as "common courtesy," but it is far from common these days. In fact, it is pretty rare. How many people do you know who follow the basic common courtesies given in this section?

A father once remarked about his three children: "My children may not be the brightest children in their class. They may not be the most talented or the most skilled. They may not achieve great fame or earn millions of dollars. But by my insisting that they have good manners, I know they will be welcome in all places and by all people." How true!

Good manners—exhibiting common courtesies—are like a calling card. They open doors that are otherwise shut to those who are rude, crude, or unmannerly. They bring welcome invitations and quite often, return engagements. They cover a multitude of weaknesses and flaws. They make other people feel good about themselves, and they in turn extend kindness and generosity they might not otherwise exhibit.

Good manners are a prerequisite for good friendships, good business associations, and good marriages. They are the key to success!

While we **have opportunity**, let us do **good** to all **people**.

GALATIONS 6:10 NASB

DON'T WORRY, BE HAPPY

Dr. Ashley Montagu met two young men shortly after the end of World War II. They had spent two years in Auschwitz, the cruel death camp operated by the Nazis. Prior to Auschwitz, they had lived in Vienna in a cellar where they had been kept hidden by Christian friends. All of the others housed with them in the cellar had been exterminated solely because they were Jews.

> **A merry heart does good, like medicine, but a broken spirit dries the bones.**
> PROVERBS 17:22 NKJV

After the war ended, these two men had walked from Vienna to Berlin, hoping to find relatives. There, they were picked up by an American Jewish soldier who brought them to America. Both of them wanted to become physicians; and that's how Dr. Montagu, a professor in a medical school, came to meet them. Noting that they "didn't exhibit any of the scars that one might have expected from their unhappy existence," he asked them how they came to be such cheerful people.

They replied, "A group of us decided that no matter what happened, it wouldn't get us down." They told him they had attempted to be cheerful regardless of their circumstances, never yielding for a moment to the idea that they were either inferior or doomed.

They were living proof to Dr. Montagu that even under impossible conditions, it's possible to be happy!

A man without mirth is like a wagon without springs; he is jolted disagreeably by every pebble in the road.

HENRY WARD BEECHER

JUST DO IT

#1

For one week, make an effort to see your circumstances from a positive perspective and make a list of the changes it makes in your life.

#2

- View your problems as challenges and opportunities.
- Force your lips to turn upwards when you feel discouraged. You will automatically feel better.
- Watch your words. Speak only positive words; avoid negative comments.

#3

- Pay attention to the mental messages you tell yourself. Change them to a positive self-statement.

#4

#5

#6

#7

#8

#9

#10

CONSIDER THIS!

Dorothy Leigh Sayers said, "Work is not primarily a thing one does to live, but the things one lives to do. It should be the full expression of the worker's faculties, the thing in which he finds spiritual, mental, and bodily satisfaction, and medium in which he offers himself to God."

Have you ever thought about work that way? As a gift from God intended to bring you satisfaction? As you consider your career options, don't settle for the job that pays the most or has the greatest status. Neither should you choose the one that requires the least effort. Continue to look until you find the one that fills you with passion, and then enjoy. That's God's formula for work.

MAKE YOUR WORK ENJOYABLE

When David was twelve, he convinced a restaurant manager that he was actually sixteen and was hired as a lunch-counter waiter for twenty-five cents an hour. The place was owned by two Greek immigrant brothers, Frank and George, who had started their lives in America as a dishwasher and hot-dog seller. David remembers that they set high standards and never asked anything of their employees that they wouldn't do themselves. Frank once told David, "As long as you try, you can always work for me. But when you don't try, you can't work for me." Trying meant everything from working hard to treating customers politely. Once, when Frank noticed a waitress giving a customer a rough time, he fired her on the spot and waited on the table himself. David determined that would never happen to him.

The usual tip for waiters in those days was a dime, but David discovered that if he brought the food out quickly and was especially polite, he sometimes got a quarter as a tip. He set a goal for himself to see how many customers he could wait on in one night. His record was one hundred!

R. David Thomas was better known as "Dave," the founder and senior chairman of Wendy's International, Inc., a chain of 4,300 restaurants.

No matter what job you do, do it well. The Bible tells us to do all our work as to the Lord (Colossians 3:23.)

> THE BIBLE KNOWS NOTHING OF A HIERARCHY OF LABOR.
> NO WORK IS DEGRADING.
> IF IT OUGHT TO BE DONE, THEN IT IS GOOD WORK.
>
> BEN PATTERSON

To receive his heritage and rejoice in his labor—this is the gift of God.

ECCLESIASTES 5:19 NKJV

HOW Do YOU MEASURE Up?

Do you have a reputation for being a hard worker, or do you tend to be a prima donna? Hopefully, you have learned how to work hard, or you are at least willing to learn. Take the following test that identifies the traits of a hard worker.

A. I offer to help when I see someone struggling with a task.
B. I do my assigned chores without my parents having to raise their voices or show the veins in their necks.
C. I earn my own spending money by working at a job outside my own home.
D. Aside from my regular chores, I volunteer to help when my family needs it. I'm a team player.
E. I pride myself in getting the best grades I am capable of.

Everyone's situation and family demands are unique, but you should be able to answer "Yes" to at least three out of the four statements above. If so, you can pat yourself on the back for being a hard worker, but don't rest on your laurels. God wants us to live passionately and give life our best effort. After we give our best, He fills in the gaps.

HARD WORK PAYS RICH DIVIDENDS

> **WHEN** YOU DO THE THINGS YOU HAVE TO DO WHEN YOU HAVE TO DO THEM, THE DAY WILL COME WHEN YOU CAN DO THE THINGS YOU WANT TO DO WHEN YOU WANT TO DO THEM.
>
> ZIG ZIGLAR

The bee is often described as being busy. It deserves this adjective! To produce one pound of honey, a bee must visit 56,000 clover heads. Since each head has sixty flower tubes, a bee must make a total of 3,360,000 visits. In the process, the average bee would travel the equivalent of three times around the world.

To make just one tablespoon of honey, the amount that might go on a biscuit, a little bee must make 4,200 trips to the flowers, averaging about ten trips a day, each trip lasting approximately twenty minutes. It visits four hundred different flowers.

Day in, day out, the work of a bee is fairly unglamorous. It flies, it takes in nectar, it flies some more, and it deposits nectar. In the process, it produces, and what it produces creates a place for it in the hive.

You may think your daily chores are a waste of time; but in fact, your completion of those chores is making you. One day, you won't even have to think: *I must get disciplined. I must get to work. I must stick with it.* If you have done your chores faithfully and to the best of your ability, the chores will have become a part of the way you tackle every challenge the rest of your life.

He who has a **slack** hand becomes **poor**, but the hand of the **diligent** makes **rich**.

PROVERBS 10:4 NKJV

RECOGNIZE WHAT HE IS CALLING YOU TO DO

One of the great disasters of history took place in 1271. In that year, Niccolo and Matteo Polo, the father and uncle of Marco Polo, visited Kubla Khan, who was considered the world ruler, with authority over all China, all India, and all of the East.

The Kubla Khan was attracted to the story of Christianity as Niccolo and Matteo told it to him. He said to them, "You shall go to your high priest and tell him on my behalf to send me a hundred men skilled in your religion and I shall be baptized, and when I am baptized all my barons and great men will be baptized and their subjects will receive baptism, too, and so there will be more Christians here than there are in your parts."

Nothing was done, however, in response to what the Kubla Khan had requested. After thirty years, only a handful of missionaries was sent. It was too few too late.

The West apparently did not have the vision to see the East won to Christ. The mind boggles at the possible ways the world might be different today if thirteenth-century China, India, and the other areas of the Orient had been converted to Christianity.

If you lack vision today, ask God for it. He has wonders to reveal to you that you can't yet imagine!

> VISION IS THE WORLD'S MOST DESPERATE NEED. THERE ARE NO PEOPLE WHO THINK HOPELESSLY.
>
> WINIFRED NEWMAN

IF PEOPLE CAN'T SEE WHAT GOD IS DOING, THEY STUMBLE ALL OVER THEMSELVES.

PROVERBS 29:18 MSG

WISE WORDS

When Jesus arrived in Capernaum, a Roman officer came and pleaded with him, "Lord, my young servant lies in bed, paralyzed and racked with pain." Jesus said, "I will come and heal him." Then the officer said, "Lord, I am not worthy to have you come into my home. Just say the word from where you are, and my servant will be healed! I know, because I am under the authority of my superior officers and I have authority over my soldiers. I only need to say, 'Go,' and they go, or 'Come,' and they come. And if I say to my slaves, 'Do this or that,' they do it."

When Jesus heard this, he was amazed. Turning to the crowd, he said, "I tell you the truth, I haven't seen faith like this in all the land of Israel!

MATTHEW 8:5-10 NLT

Additional copies of this book are available
from your local bookstore.

The following titles are also available:

Pocket Guide for Teens
Be Patient, God's Not Finished with Me Yet (Teen Edition)
Truth Unplugged for Girls
Truth Unplugged for Boys

If you have enjoyed this book,
or if it has impacted your life,
we would like to hear from you.

Please contact us at:

Honor Books,
An Imprint of Cook Communications Ministries
4050 Lee Vance View
Colorado Springs, CO 80918
www.cookministries.org